Holy War for True Democracy

Holy War for True Democracy

Powered by Passion and Technology

Jon Ferraiolo

Jon Ferraiolo Publishing
JonFPublishing@ferraiolo.com,
855 El Camino Real, Suite 13A-157
Palo Alto CA 94301-2326

Cover design by Dragan Bilic

FIRST EDITION

Library of Congress Control Number: 2017904221

Print ISBN: 978-0-692-89417-0

Ebook ISBN: 978-1-5323-3633-1

PRINTED IN THE UNITED STATES OF AMERICA

Contents

To Karen

1 Has Democracy Lost Its Fervor?

Now, more than ever, our democracies and the shared understanding of truth on which they rely are under threat. A major factor is the complacency and cynicism of many who take for granted the freedoms we enjoy, forgetting the sacrifices our ancestors made:

- Countless Wars of Independence and revolutions in the 18th and 19th centuries, including America, France and Latin America

- A great American Civil War that ended the practice of men enslaving other men

- World War II (withs tens of millions dying), which enabled Western democracies to survive against the attempted world domination by authoritarian military dictatorships

- In India, Gandhi helped to end centuries of Colonial Rule by leading a revolt centered on passive resistance, resulting in the world's largest democracy

- Western democracies waged a forty-year Cold War against the brutal and oppressive Soviet Union

- Decades of struggle finally ended Apartheid in South Africa, bringing democracy to all the people of that country

The above bullets highlight some of the sacrifices, fueled by passion, that have resulted in our ability to govern ourselves and enjoy our freedoms.

Have we lost our former passion for self-government? Many contemporary thought leaders are concerned:

> "We do not yet face a cataclysm like that of the late 1930s. But our era is coming to resemble that one when the democratic powers lost their moral fervor, their self-confidence, their military edge, and the will to use their power against aggression whose ultimate target was the international order itself."
> [1][2]

> "The world in 2015 was battered by overlapping crises that contributed to the 10th consecutive year of decline in global freedom." [3]

"How Stable Are Democracies? 'Warning Signs Are Flashing Red'". [4]

This book argues that we cannot take our hard-fought democratic freedoms for granted because, if we do, a demagogue will emerge who will take advantage of today's centralization of modern media and the Internet to convince enough of us to willingly vote to relinquish all political control to a powerful few, who will then improve their lives at our expense.

Instead, we need to undergo the equivalent of a Holy War to save democracy from falling into a totalitarian autocratic state monitored by pervasive electronic surveillance where we lose the freedoms we have today – the freedoms to believe as we wish, say what we think, do as we want and love whom we choose – basically, to be in charge of our own lives, rather than being subservient to an oppressive paranoid military dictatorship like North Korea, a nationalist billionaire oligarchy like Russia or a religious autocracy like some countries in the Middle East. Furthermore, if we want democracy to survive for generations, not only do we need to establish defenses against today's threats, we need to strengthen our democratic institutions by mobilizing passion and technology to protect against future threats.

IS THIS BOOK LIBERAL OR CONSERVATIVE?

This book is neither liberal or conservative. The book does not have an opinion about universal health care, nuclear proliferation or tax policy.

But the author is passionate about governments serving its citizens to the utmost. I want governments to serve all people as fairly and equally as possible. I desperately want to prevent government from oppression against its own people. I also desperately want to prevent a subset of the people taking advantage of power (e.g., money) to influence government (and public sentiment) to their advantage at the expense of the less powerful.

DOES THIS BOOK ADVOCATE A PARTICULAR POLITICAL SYSTEM, E.G., DEMOCRACY?

Even though the book's title is "Holy War for True Democracy", this book does not advocate that any countries change their political systems. The approaches described here (except for some future ideas in Chapter 7) can work with any political system, including dictatorships. The book outlines a set of techniques that can be superimposed on any political system so long as the government truly sees its primary mission as promoting the welfare of all of its people, rather than enriching a subset at the expense of others, or preserving government power at the expense of the people.

DOES THIS BOOK ADVOCATE A PARTICULAR RELIGION?

The title starts with "Holy War... . ", but the book is independent of religion.

The book does embrace a set of commonly-held principles that include religious tolerance. Therefore, the book might conflict with some religious groups who advocate intolerance toward other religious points of view.

The use of the term Holy War conveys the dedication, fervor, and, on occasion, sacrifice that is necessary to fight off selfish interest in order to achieve governments that optimize life for all citizens rather than just the powerful few.

ORGANIZATION OF THIS BOOK

The first chapters highlight what is at stake and the urgency of the problem:

Chapter 2 – An Age-Old Conflict: Highlights threats to democracy today (early 2017), and then takes a step backward to show that government institutions are always evolving – often: out with the old, in with the new.

Chapter 3 – Threat of Big Brother: Identifies the biggest threats to democracy which have the greatest potential to move us toward the dystopian future described in George Orwell's "1984".

Chapter 4 – True Democracy: Offers the author's definition of a true democracy. Then, looks at democratic systems throughout history and where they've fallen short of truly representing their citizens.

Chapter 5 – Holy War: A call to action to fight for true democracy with fervor. It lays the groundwork for the principles that a truly democratic society should strive for and why passion is critical.

The next two chapters provide concrete proposals for human and technological solutions:

Chapter 6 – Prioritizing Trustworthiness: Begins with a study on trust in society. Then it presents a specific plan to promote trustworthy information on government and politics by setting up a crowd-sourced trustworthiness online service that leverages modern social media techniques to pressure politicians, government representatives and the media to publish the whole truth and nothing but the truth, unbiased and without distortion.

Chapter 7 – Towards True Democracy: Describes Democracy Guardians (DG), a nonprofit that would administer the trustworthiness initiative. DG would also take on other initiatives to fortify today's representative democracies and move the world gradually towards true democracy.

The last chapter provides final thoughts:

Chapter 8 – Conclusion – Calls to Action: Concludes with a summation of what we need to do to make democratic self-government survive and thrive well into the future.

2 An Age-Old Conflict

This book was written in early 2017, soon after the inauguration of Donald J. Trump as the 45th President of the United States. The inauguration drew a large crowd of Trump supporters who hope Trump will be a revolutionary force against the Western liberal order, which some believe is destroying their beliefs and way of living. Trump rode a worldwide movement centered on nationalist populism and extreme right-wing ideology to win more Electoral College votes than his Democratic opponent, even though Mrs. Clinton won the popular vote by nearly three million.

The day after the inauguration, even greater crowds (more than two million in approximately 650 different cities worldwide) came out to protest against Trump in what was called the Women's March on Washington. [1] The protests were remarkable in that they were spontaneous, grassroots activism in response to a tweet from a Hawaiian woman in her sixties. [2] In general, the protesters are more positive about the Western liberal order. Unlike Trump, they generally accept a rapidly changing world, both technology changes (e.g., computers and automation) and social changes (e.g., non-whites and LGBTQ). They tend to believe that government has a role in regulating the marketplace to prevent abuses and ensure equal opportunity.

One major issue in the presidential campaign was "fake news", where seemingly legitimate news articles contained outright lies.[3] [4] [5] The Trump supporters claimed the mainstream media were biased, [6] whereas the liberals countered that Trump supporters in America, Russia and elsewhere published fake news articles that liberals claimed were instrumental in giving Trump an electoral victory. [7]

It seems like there are two realities. For example, after the Women's March, there was a big debate about how many people attended the Trump inauguration. The Trump team claimed it was the biggest inaugural crowd ever, [8] but the mainstream media pushed back with photographs that appeared to show crowds considerably smaller than the 2009 inauguration. [9] Then, a spokeswoman for Trump said they were just presenting "alternative facts", as if there are two realities, both equally valid. [10]

Clearly, we are in the midst of an assault on truth, and are experiencing a major clash over whether the Western liberal order is generally beneficial or harmful.

Assaults on truth are nothing new. Trailblazing scientists in the past have been persecuted, jailed, tortured and occasionally killed by people in power who felt threatened by emerging science. A famous case in point is Galileo, who angered the Church by stating that his telescope observations confirmed that the Earth revolves around the sun. Because the Catholic Church felt threatened, he was convicted and spent his last years under house arrest. His scientific papers were banned. More recently, the Canadian government of Stephen Harper (2006-2015) was accused of censoring climate scientists. [11]

Disagreement on whether political change is good or bad is also an age-old conflict. Let's take the history of slavery as a case in point. Thousands of years ago slavery was common across most of the globe, and few people questioned the morality of slavery – it was the status quo. But as civilization evolved, people changed the world order to outlaw slavery bit by bit. In the USA, there was a great Civil War in the 1860s over slavery. Only after that war was slavery unlawful. To me, this is just one example of the new world order (abolitionists) vs. the old world order (slave owners). Readers will agree that the new world order was right on slavery.

Another example is Marxism, which believed that industrial society would quickly evolve into a dictatorship of the proletariat (working class). In this case, the proposed new world order was socialism, and the old world order was capitalism. The West generally rejected Marxism and stuck with capitalism. Some countries still embrace aspects of Marxism, but nearly every country takes advantage of free markets today for all or part of their economies. Therefore, readers will agree that Marx's proposed new world order was ultimately rejected or at least severely modified by most countries, which shows that new does not always prevail.

Technology and knowledge are often the primary drivers for changes to the existing world order. For example, technology advances contributed to the increase in rights for women, including suffrage. Before the first Industrial Revolution, many women in the West had to spin their own thread, weave their own cloth and sew their own clothes. As manufactured clothes became popular, and with the advent of many other similar advances, women had more time and greater ability to engage in activities, including voting, that previously were the domain of men. Women's suffrage is now the law almost everywhere in the world. [12]

Similarly, transportation and communications advances

have been prime drivers of the huge growth in globalization in recent decades.

Even more fundamental is the gradual acceptance of free enterprise in the world order. Some pillars of free enterprise only became accepted in fairly recent times. For example, modern corporations, modern banking and stock markets were 19th century inventions. Few people today believe we should turn back the clock on corporations and banks, although there is major disagreement about how much governments should regulate corporations and banks.

The Hegelian dialectic [13] of thesis, antithesis and synthesis continues in the world today. Society is highly dynamic due to technology change and the collective knowledge and experience of mankind. Technology and knowledge drive changes in attitudes, including our attitudes toward government and politics.

3 Threat of Big Brother

Many readers will know the premise of George Orwell's dystopian novel *1984* (published in 1949), which describes a futuristic world where an authoritarian government monitors your movements, actions and even your ideas (via the Thought Police). All around are signs saying "Big Brother is watching you." There are three major powers, Oceania (presumably centered on USA and UK), Eurasia (presumably centered on the Soviet Union) and Eastasia (presumably centered on China), who are extremely nationalistic and constantly at war. The novel has become a best-seller again in 2017 in the first days of the Trump presidency because some people see parallels. [1]

Skeptics about the threat of Big Brother might argue that it has been almost seven decades since the book was published and people in the West are still free. Further, they might say authoritarian regimes never last, citing a handful of examples: Mussolini was dragged through the streets of Italy; Hitler shot himself in a bunker to avoid capture; Stalin's brutal Soviet Union ultimately collapsed in 1989; and Mao's China ultimately granted much more freedom to its people.

However, I believe the free countries of the world are now in grave danger of falling into the clutches of an authoritarian government which monitors and controls us using Big Brother-like surveillance. In the rest of the chapter, I will explain why I believe people of the free world need to mount the equivalent of a Holy War or else our freedoms will be taken away forever.

THE OPPORTUNITY FOR OPPRESSION USING TECHNOLOGY

In 2013, Edward Snowden released a massive collection of classified documents from the US intelligence services that revealed extraordinary global surveillance programs that, among other things, collected daily phone records with the help of major phone companies, tracked people's cell phone location, collected people's contact lists and spied on foreign leaders, including allies such as German Chancellor Angela Merkel. [2][3] Snowden claimed that as an NSA analyst, "I, sitting at my desk, [could] wiretap anyone, from you or your accountant, to a federal judge or even the president, if I had a personal email." [4] Among the documents was a slide deck that said NSA's objective was to "Collect it All," "Process it All," "Exploit it All," "Partner it All," "Sniff it All" and "Know it All." [5] Many of these surveillance programs were authorized by the Patriot Act, which was approved by Congress during a period of fear among the American people by legislators who were trying to keep the country safe. [6]

Note that the NSA global surveillance programs were launched in the wake of 9/11 to try to discover and thwart future terrorist attacks, and thereby keep the American people safe. Although we cannot know all of the actions and motivations of the US intelligence services, my personal judgment, based on lack of news reports about political or financial abuses, is that the Bush and Obama administrations generally used the NSA programs for combating terrorism rather than oppressing the American people. But these programs show how easy it is today for governments to do Big Brother-like surveillance on its people and how easily leaders can convince citizens to surrender their privacy. All it takes is one strong charismatic demagogue who believes he has a divine mission or the right ideology or is simply a megalomaniac; who has a convenient trigger event such as a terrorist attack that alarms citizens; and then decides it is his right or duty to spy on and oppress his citizens. An oppressive government could require the technology companies to share all user activity. This is not a paranoid rant. Snowden showed that large technology companies have already cooperated with the NSA. [7]

It is important to remember all of the surveillance tools that are available to oppressive governments. Everything we do on our cell phones is controlled by a small number of telecommunications network providers and cell phone manufacturers who can be easily coerced into cooperating with the government. The cell phone has a record of all our contacts and all communications with others. Our phone GPS tracks where we are at all times. Self-driving cars will notify cloud-based navigation services where your vehicle is. Nearly every purchase is done with credit or debit cards, so an oppressive government can coerce banks to share every purchase you make. Google and Facebook already share information about you with advertisers; [8] an oppressive government can demand that these companies share all your email and social media or else face fines or even threaten to stop the company from doing business. Some countries like the UK already have extensive surveillance cameras throughout major cities, set up for counterterrorism.[9] Facial recognition software is amazingly good these days and is only getting better.

In the following sections, I list the various triggers that a demagogue might use to convince people in free countries to grant his government strong surveillance powers that the government could abuse at the expense of the people's freedoms.

FEAR OF TERRORISM

As everyone knows, the NSA surveillance programs were a reaction to the horrifying Al Qaeda attacks of 9/11. In 2015 and 2016, there were a series of ISIS-planned attacks in Europe and the Middle East, and there were a number of lone wolf mass murders in the US, some inspired by ISIS or Al Qaeda.

There are many people in the West who fear all Muslims. This fear contributed to the Brexit victory and to Donald Trump's election. On December 7, 2015, Trump said this: "Donald J. Trump is calling for a total and complete shutdown of Muslims entering the United States until our country's representatives can figure out what the hell is going on", thereby demonizing 1.6 billion Muslims worldwide. Just 9 days after taking office, President Trump signed an executive order temporarily banning entry from seven Muslim countries to keep America safe and fulfill a campaign promise, even though no Americans have ever been killed by people coming to America from those countries. [10] Therefore, even without history of violence against Americans, these countries were singled out because of concerns about the potential for terrorism due to political instability (which might allow extremism to grow) and because they are predominantly Muslim.

The 9/11 attacks led to two wars, one in Afghanistan and one in Iraq, and a huge surveillance program. Recent domestic terrorist attacks by radicalized Muslims likely led to the Muslim ban executive order. What happens after the next terrorist attack on US soil by a self-radicalized Muslim citizen, given Trump's desire to appear as a strong leader? It would not be surprising if invasive domestic surveillance programs were strengthened.

Clearly, another major terrorist attack on American soil would likely trigger another round of government surveillance, and perhaps other actions, such as a Muslim registry. Once in place, the ruling party might leverage the surveillance apparatus for political purposes, initially rationalizing that only they can keep the country safe, and then rationalizing that it was their duty to rig future elections.

NATIONALISM

Closely related to terrorism fears is the recent growth of popular sentiment for nationalism and against globalism. Brexit represented a nationalist vote by the people of Great Britain to withdraw from the European Union and go it alone. In America, one of Trump's slogans was "America First", which indicates a selfish desire to withdraw from world leadership so that America can focus on "winning". In western Europe, right-wing nationalist candidates have a good shot at victory in some countries later in 2017.

Clearly, in the UK, USA and western Europe, many of the same people who support nationalism do so largely out of fear or resentment of immigrants with different skin color or religion than the established Christian white majorities. There is an element of scapegoating, where politicians blame the immigrants who look different for all sorts of problems, including terrorism, crime, taking away jobs and costing taxpayer money. There are enough people who feel this fear that these nationalists are winning key elections, such as President of the United States.

There are other dark sides to nationalism. Nationalism, and its companion militarism, were prime causes of World War I. [11] It was also a major factor in the rise of the Nazis, and thus a key contributor to World War II. [12] Nazi Germany was a police state, where the Gestapo watched over all citizens. [13] Nazi Germany scapegoated the Jews, first creating a registry, then sending them to concentration camps and ultimately killing six million people. [14]

If put in power, nationalist politicians often persecute any detractors, labeling them as enemies of the state. [15][16] Nationalists also try to control the press, where criticism is characterized as unpatriotic. Clearly, if a nationalist government is interested in controlling the press, they would also be more than happy to go further, all the way to Big Brother tactics.

FOREIGN GOVERNMENTS UNDERMINING DEMOCRACY

As stated previously, the US government has concluded that the Russian government sponsored a coordinated attack on the 2016 presidential election. [17] The UK has similarly concluded that the Russians interfered with the 2016 vote about whether the UK should withdraw from the European Union. [18] This Russian effort extends across many European and Western Asian countries, including many countries that used to be part of the Soviet Union. [19] Among the Russian goals are to undermine democracy, break up NATO and the European Union and thereby have the opportunity to either take over neighboring countries or have hegemony over them – basically to restore the glories of the Russian Empire or the Soviet Union. [20][21]

This is not the first time that despots wanted self-government to fail. At the time of the American Civil War, most governments of Europe were autocratic, with many monarchies still present. Many European citizens wanted to bring down the autocratic governments and install constitutional democracies with freedoms like those present in America. Obviously, this was a major threat to the autocrats, some of whom actively explored how to help the South. This would have severely weakened the American experiment in democracy and would have greatly depressed the momentum for European democratic movements. Ultimately, the South lost, the American nation was preserved, and European democracy advocates displaced many autocracies with constitutional democracies in subsequent decades. [22]

If democracy fails, despots will take over. The world will be run by people like Vladimir Putin who will use all available tools, including surveillance, to preserve their power.

BIG BUSINESS AND THE RICH

We are in the era of giant multinational companies and billionaires. Wealth and power are concentrated in the hands of a few people. [23] Furthermore, most of the media in the US is controlled by a few mega corporations (e.g., Time-Warner, News Corp, GE, Viacom and CBS). [24]

The wealthy, and the giant companies that some of them manage, have the opportunity to control politicians via campaign donations and to control public opinion, particularly if they manage to acquire media organizations. Many American liberals believe this has already happened to some extent via billionaires providing major funding for the Republican party and their alleged propaganda machine, Fox News. I personally believe there is only a partial truth here, and similar charges can be made of the Democrats. The wealthiest Americans do use their money to influence politics, but they try to influence both parties. If they give more on average to Republicans, it's most often because wealthy people tend to agree ideologically with the Republican party, just as labor unions historically have been big Democratic donors because they tend to agree ideologically with Democratic policy. The money advantage probably tends to go to the Republicans because wealthy people have more money to spend influencing politics. Regarding Fox News, it appears to be a mixed bag between honest journalism and Republican propaganda. I once had a talk with a graduate student recently from mainland China who said the Chinese government should study Fox News for better techniques in how to control its people.

I don't believe that big business and billionaires will take over the USA imminently. A takeover would require a billionaire demagogue who wants big business and the wealthy to exercise totalitarian control. Instead, today we have billionaire Donald Trump who sees rust belt workers as a key constituency and has a political agenda that deviates somewhat from the Republican billionaire donors. [25]

Nevertheless, there is an opportunity for a megalomaniac rich person with leverage over key media outlets to assume power and leverage global surveillance and media propaganda to preserve and enhance that power. A contemporary example is Silvio Berlusconi (1994-1995,

2001-2006, 2008-2011) who used his media empire to hold on to power in Italy. [26]

RELIGIOUS FUNDAMENTALISM

Predominantly Muslim nations have shown the risk of religious fundamentalists taking over the government. In this scenario, people voluntarily entrust a leader with religious credentials with extraordinary governing power, such as what is currently happening in Erdogan's Turkey, where a century of democracy is in danger.[27]

Some members of the Right also worry about a mass influx of Islamic refugees leading to destruction of Western civilization, and perhaps introduction of Sharia law. [28]

Predominantly Christian countries seem to be out of imminent danger of a Christian religious government takeover. It has happened in the past, such as Oliver Cromwell's Puritan government in England in the mid 1600s, but in modern times other threats are more worrisome.

CLIMATE-DRIVEN HAVOC (REFUGEES, FOOD SHORTAGES, DISEASE, ETC.)

Contrary to popular perception, serious scientists who devote their careers to studying climate change generally do not absolutely believe that mankind is the one and only cause of dramatic climate change, such as global warming;

instead, climate scientists observe various alarming indicators (warming average temperatures, [29]warming oceans, [30] melting polar ice, [31] rising oceans, [32] migrating or disappearing species, etc.) and attempt to explain these phenomena by careful scientific study. [33]

Scientists have reached consensus opinions, based on decades of research and discussion of these various phenomena, that some climate changes are explained by the ever-changing natural world (e.g., fluctuations in solar activity, volcanoes, changes in Earth's orbit or magnetic fields, and simple random chance); some are currently unexplainable and require further study; and others are best explained by mankind affecting the planet as a side-effect of industrialization, technology advances and human population growth.

The greenhouse effect (actually, the *growing* greenhouse effect) is the most famous phenomenon that scientists generally believe is primarily due to human activity. Scientific observation shows a sharp increase in certain atmospheric gases, particularly carbon dioxide, and these gases (due to the unique characteristics of their molecular vibrations and rotations) happen to block a percentage of infrared rays (i.e., heat) from escaping into space. [34] We have always had carbon dioxide in the atmosphere, and therefore there has always been a greenhouse effect. What concerns climate scientists and world leaders today is that carbon dioxide levels are nearing unprecedented levels, [35] trapping more planetary heat, thereby raising temperatures, melting ice caps and raising ocean levels (partly due to water expansion at higher temperatures), among other catastrophic developments. [36]

The data used in the climate models has been painstakingly gathered by experts over decades and reviewed with scientific rigor by other experts. Some of the data holds atmospheric levels of oxygen and carbon dioxide going back hundreds of millions of years pulled from the polar regions where glaciers have captured air bubbles from Earth's distant past. [37] Ocean temperatures from distant times have been determined by studying the chemical makeup of ancient fossils. [38][39]Historical sea levels are easily discovered by the same geology techniques that tell us the age of the Grand Canyon. From many other similar data sources, various teams of scientists and mathematicians have used Big Data techniques to independently develop computer models to see which ones best predict global climate change from the ancient past to the present.

Some scientists and mathematicians focus on more recent climate history, such as the last thousand years or the last fifty years. They use other similar techniques to gather more recent historical climate data and develop computer models that fit the data.

Then the scientists use the same predictive mathematical techniques that businesses use to predict expected sales or that meteorologists use to predict the weather. Several different groups each has its own computer models that produce different predictions. The scientists are meticulous because science is a solemn activity. Your reputation and livelihood (even your will to live [40]) could be destroyed if you are discovered to be an unreliable scientist.

So, many climate scientists believe the Earth has been warming alarmingly quickly in the last two decades, that ocean temperatures are rising, glaciers are melting and ice caps are melting. [41] It is possible that these phenomena might reinforce each other to multiply the speed of rising temperatures and oceans: warmer oceans melt the ice caps faster, which then cause smaller ice caps to reflect less sunlight, and cause oceans to warm further. Climate change might not happen, it might happen gradually or it might happen dramatically and catastrophically.

I hope mankind gets lucky and we can avoid global catastrophe, but at a minimum, scientists generally believe we will end up with some major problems nevertheless, possibly including tens of millions displaced people needing a new place to live [42]; local weather changes disrupting agriculture on a massive scale causing food and water shortages and wreaking havoc with world economies; or new germs that are unleashed due to major environmental changes [43]. It is highly likely that something bad will happen to many people sooner or later as a result of human-induced climate change; we just can't predict exactly what will happen and in what time frame. Starving people will do desperate things. People who have been spared the worst effects will argue about how selfish or compassionate they should be, which might translate into whether to let millions of others suffer.

The Big Brother danger is that a leader emerges and promises to wall off the country from refugees, and uses the crisis to justify powers that allow him to create a police state.

OTHER THINGS

Many readers will say I left out other eventualities that might lead to loss of democratic rule. For example, science getting too enamored with advancement and inadvertently creating new superbugs or invasive insects via genetic engineering; or the old classic about robots taking over. There is also the possibility of a new weapon such as an army of nano-drones that a Dr. Evil creates to bring all of mankind under his rule.

Outside of science fiction scenarios, there is always the threat of global natural disaster, such as a huge volcanic eruption that covers the skies with soot, a series of colossal earthquakes or an asteroid hitting the Earth such as what happened at the end of the dinosaur era. Another possibility is nuclear bombs disrupting the world order, either from a terrorist group or a nation led by a crazed leader.

I feel these other scenarios are much less likely to occur, but there are many ways the world order can be shaken, which would cause democracy to be threatened.

4 True Democracy

TRUE DEMOCRACY DEFINED

In mankind's history, we have never had a True Democracy, which I define as follows:

- Every single adult citizen has the right to vote

- Citizenship is available on an equal basis to all adults regardless of race, ethnicity, gender, economic status or political inclination so long as the given adult meets a set of fair citizenship criteria that are not prejudicial against any particular group

- Citizens vote directly on elected government positions (e.g., President) and on legislation, rather than indirectly via elected representatives (i.e., direct democracy)

- All citizens are fully informed by science-based and objective facts and analysis. Commercial and political special interests are not able to manipulate the views of the voters except through fact-based information that simultaneously shows all sides of the discussion fairly and respectfully.

The above definition represents an aspirational ideal which probably can never be achieved completely. However, I believe that with passion, effort and persistence, certain countries of the world can ultimately come very close to True Democracy. Every bit of progress towards the ideal represents a greater fulfillment of the democratic notion of government of the people, by the people and for the people.

DEMOCRACY THROUGHOUT HISTORY

Ancient Greece might not have been the first democracy in history, but it is the earliest one for which we have detailed knowledge.

The Athenian democracy was at its peak between 507 BC and 328 BC, when Alexander the Great conquered them. It is considered a direct democracy because the people voted directly on issues. Citizenship was only for men who had completed military training, which meant that only 10-20% of its 100,000-300,000 inhabitants were citizens. The Athenians, like nearly every state at the time, practiced slavery.

Here is a quote from Socrates (470-399 BC) about

Athenian democracy and individual liberty from Aristotle's *Politics*:

> Now a fundamental principle of the democratic form
> of constitution is liberty—that is what is usually
> asserted, implying that only under this constitution
> do men participate in liberty, for they assert this as
> the aim of every democracy. But one factor of liberty
> is to govern and be governed in turn; for the popular
> principle of justice is to have equality according to
> number, not worth, and if this is the principle of
> justice prevailing, the multitude must of necessity be
> sovereign and the decision of the majority must be
> final and must constitute justice, for they say that
> each of the citizens ought to have an equal share; so
> that it results that in democracies the poor are more
> powerful than the rich, because there are more of
> them and whatever is decided by the majority is
> sovereign. This then is one mark of liberty which all
> democrats set down as a principle of the constitution.
> And one is for a man to live as he likes; for they say
> that this is the function of liberty, inasmuch as to live
> not as one likes is the life of a man that is a slave.
> This is the second principle of democracy, and from
> it has come the claim not to be governed, preferably
> not by anybody, or failing that, to govern and be
> governed in turns; and this is the way in which the

second principle contributes to equalitarian liberty.
[1]

The Roman Republic lasted from 509-27 BC. Whereas Athens had a direct democracy, Rome had a representative democracy with two main groups, the patricians (wealthy landowners) and the plebeians (all other citizens) constantly fighting for power. The Roman Republic had a complex approach that tried to include checks and balances on power, but many times the powerful few were able to dictate to the masses.

In the Middle Ages, there were various governments that had democratic features, such as the Republic of Venice, which was a mixture of rule by a despot (the doge), an aristocracy and a limited role for the other citizens. Florence also was technically a democracy, but in practice ruling families like the Medici usually held most of the power.

England had a gradual march towards representative democracy starting with the Magna Carta of 1215 AD, which forced the king to share power with the most powerful nobles. This document hardly represented True Democracy, and the Magna Carta was ignored by subsequent kings. Nevertheless, it became a rallying call for future generations to dilute the power of the king and give increasing power over time to Parliament. By the nineteenth century, England was effectively a representative democracy.

Which brings us to the American experiment in democracy. The Founding Fathers, greatly influenced by the Enlightenment, were highly educated and studied democracies and republics throughout history to figure out the optimal approach. They then had to balance ideals against the various self-interests of the thirteen colonies when drafting the US Constitution.

America at the time of the first Congress and Presidency (1789) was hardly a True Democracy. At this time, most states only allowed white, male property owners to vote. Within subsequent decades, states allowed all white males to vote. Never a direct democracy, instead it was a federal republic. It was federal because of strong states' rights. It was a republic because the people elected representatives to vote on legislation. Blacks were granted the right to vote in 1870 and women in 1920, but it wasn't until the Voting Rights Act (1965) that nearly every adult effectively had full voting rights. Other factors that keep America from being a True Democracy include the US Senate, which gives smaller states greater legislative power than warranted by their populations, and the Electoral College, which gives greater electoral power in choosing the President to smaller population states. Today, the USA is still far from a true democracy.

The twentieth century saw the rise of many constitutional representative democracies across the world. Most studied the early democracies, such as USA, UK and France, in writing their constitutions. Some countries today have successful democracies which do a good job of fulfilling the promise of the people, by the people and for the people. However, others are highly imperfect because the powerful few have disproportionate control over the many. Some countries call themselves democracies, but the government restricts freedoms to the point that the country operates as a dictatorship rather than a democracy. [2] Even in the USA today, although all citizens supposedly can vote, the combination of fake news, [3] gerrymandering [4] and voter suppression [5] threaten the democratic process.

WHAT'S WRONG WITH REPRESENTATIVE DEMOCRACY

Most constitutional democracies in the world today are representative democracies where citizens elect representatives who will draft and vote on legislation or execute the laws of the country. Except for binding referendums, such as the California Proposition system, [6] voters do not vote directly on laws.

The main problems with representative democracy are that our elected representatives are a huge leverage point which the powerful few can use at the expense of the many:

- **Outright bribes and favors.** Outright bribery is less prevalent in the leading countries in the West, but it still happens everywhere. In countries that enforce their anti-bribery laws, special interests will channel money and favors in ways that either circumvent the law or are difficult to trace.

- **Campaign contributions.** Powerful self-interests can control legislators via "legal bribes" [7] (e.g., campaign contributions) and "legal blackmail" (e.g., threatening to give contributions to opposing candidates). In the USA, presidential campaigns cost at least a billion dollars, with much more campaign finance money coming from corporations and the richest Americans than from ordinary citizens. (The Citizens United decision by the Supreme Court allows unlimited contributions from corporations.[8]) Candidates run for office both for selfish and altruistic reasons. The primary selfish goals are the thrill of having power, ego gratification, personal inertia (particularly with incumbents) and financial gain, usually future income from leveraging your knowledge and connections to become a lobbyist or consultant after leaving office. Most candidates are motivated by one of the following: their careers and financial well-being, perhaps driven by a motivation to be a good provider; or they need to simply feed their egos; or they simply believe they are on the right side of policy issues and have a moral obligation to serve. For all of these scenarios, the candidate needs money and connections to get elected, and the people who give contributions expect a return on investment. One glaring example of campaign contributions attempting to directly influence votes is the March 2017 announcement by the Koch Brothers of a huge campaign fund that would only be available to legislators who voted "no" on a particular piece of legislation. [9]

- **Campaign threats.** In the USA, 85% of voters are in favor of minor changes to gun laws to require background checks on all gun sales. [10] However, such legislation cannot get enacted because the National Rifle Association will attack any candidate that advocates even the smallest impediment to purchasing guns. [11][12] Another example is the AARP's ability to discourage politicians from even hinting at senior citizen entitlement reform despite impending insolvency of Social Security and Medicare. [13]

- **Lobbying.** Powerful self-interests tip the scales in government by using their deep pockets to hire the world's best lobbyists to persuade people in government to act in ways that serve them, not the citizens at large.

- **Revolving door.** Often, people who once worked for

government as either an elected or appointed official will be employed by big companies or lobbying firms. Knowledge of this possibility may factor into some government officials' minds and affect their decisions – a person may choose to avoid taking action that a future employer might not like. Note that both Obama and Trump have taken action where they claim to address aspects of this problem. [14]

- **Hidden money.** In the USA, superPACs and 527 organizations [15] provide ways that big money can influence politics without attribution, thereby allowing candidates and causes to appear independent of special interests even if it is not true.

- **One candidate, many issues.** When citizens choose a candidate in a country with only two major political parties, they have to choose the candidate that best matches their priorities. Often voters like one candidate's position on some issues but the other candidate's position on other issues. For example, I tend to be liberal on social issues but conservative on spending, deficits and national security so I am usually conflicted when I vote between the liberal and conservative candidates, and usually unhappy with some of either candidate's votes once they get into office.

- **Slanted media.** For any democracy, the media plays a vital role in educating the citizenry about key issues facing government. Journalism schools emphasize the need for unbiased, fact-based reporting with confirmation from multiple sources. Many journalists take these responsibilities seriously, but the powerful few recognize the power of the media and try their best to influence the opinions of the populace, even to the point of buying TV networks and newspapers. [16] In the 2016 Presidential election in the USA, according to US intelligence agencies, the Russian government purposely tried to tip the election to Donald Trump by a slow drip of anti-Clinton leaks that dominated the election news cycle. [17] Therefore, even if the media sincerely tries to be fair, they can be manipulated by clever people who create sensational headlines to cause coverage slanted in their favor.

- **Social media echo chamber.** In the USA election of 2016, for the first time ever, we saw a major impact from social media, particularly Facebook. Many people now get much of their political news from Facebook, where they primarily interact with friends and family who share the same political outlook, thereby diminishing their exposure to other points of view and promoting an us vs them attitude. The echo chamber promotes divisiveness and emotion. The problem is compounded by a lack of information literacy, and our increased propensity to trust people that we know, even on topics about which they know nothing. [18]

Politicians are now using advanced data analytics to send personalized Facebook news articles to specific individuals in their base in order to fortify their commitment, which as a consequence increases divisiveness. [19]

Many of the shortcomings of representative democracy is the natural formation of political parties. The framers of the US Constitution warned us against the dangers of political parties. [20][21]

True Democracy as described in this book will address all of the above shortcomings.

IS DEMOCRACY OVERDUE FOR AN UPDATE?

The United States Constitution was written in 1787, a long time ago. The Founding Fathers did an amazing job laying the groundwork for the American experiment in democracy. It is now 240 years later and the Constitution is still the law of the land. Similar constitutions support democratic governments across the world, with widely varying success in terms of fulfilling the promise of the people, by the people and for the people. Some democracies do a good job of serving their citizens, but unfortunately many democracies concentrate power in a privileged few.

We have learned a lot about constitutions and democracies since 1787. Some newer countries have studied and learned from older democracies, and have adjusted the checks and balances to achieve more effective and less corrupt governments.

But in other cases, the powerful few have figured out how to take advantage of representative democracy to further their own selfish interests (usually, financial power or ideology). Some democracies are far from true because the government controls the media and imprisons or assassinates those who oppose. Even in some of the more true democracies, the powerful few use various techniques to stack the process in their favor, such as: illegal bribes and threats; legal versions of bribes and threats, such as campaign donations or career help to a family member; hiring the best lawyers and lobbyists; and either controlling the media via ownership or manipulating the media by hiring the best political communications firms. In 2016, we saw a new way to disrupt democracy via Russian state-sponsored hacking and fake news articles. [22]

So, democracy is working today in many countries, but with many imperfections.

I don't agree that any constitution, American or otherwise, is sacred like religions treat their sacred texts. Constitutions are written by humans. Humans are fallible and self-interested. All constitutions required compromise, and often the powerful few made sure the constitution had provisions that were in their favor. For example, the

American Constitution embraced slavery and includes features to prevent future slavery abolition, including a clause where each slave counted as three-fifths of a voter so that slave states would have more control over the House of Representatives and Electoral College than they would deserve based on number of enfranchised voters. Slavery was abolished later by Constitutional amendment, but only after a horrific civil war where the winning side (the Union) temporarily disenfranchised most Southern whites, which allowed the amendment to be approved. Therefore, I reject characterizations that constitutions are somehow divine or sacred.

The world is much different today than when the US Constitution was written in 1787. Here are some major changes that have radically changed life in ways that could not have been foreseen by Madison, Hamilton and the other Founding Fathers:

- The Industrial Revolution of the 19th century, which transformed the West from agrarianism to industrialism. With that came job specialization, the need for universal education, mass migrations to major population centers, concentration of wealth, brutal working conditions, the era of petrochemicals and environmental crises.

- The American Civil War, which eliminated slavery and kept the Union together, also remade American government. The centralized Union command during the war evolved into much greater federal power over the states, starting the path to big government. America changed from a federal union of largely independent states into a powerful centralized nation.

- After the Civil War, blacks were no longer slaves, but discrimination and oppression continued. Jim Crow laws in the South (and continuing racial prejudice everywhere) prevented true equality. Even today, racism and bigotry are still rampant around the world. We have learned that constitutional democracy does not necessarily lead to equality.

- Women's suffrage movements of the late 19th century led to women's right to vote in the early 20th century.

- In the late 19th century, the industrialized West saw great concentration of wealth in a handful of businessmen who brutally eliminated competitors and exploited workers, and thereby built great monopolies. This led to the reactions of populism and trust busting, leveling the marketplace playing field somewhat. From this we learned that technology change provides opportunity for abuse by the powerful few.

- One of the main causes of World War I was excessive nationalism, which we now know can lead to unfathomable horror.

- We learned from the Roaring Twenties and the

ensuing Great Depression that unfettered capitalism will ultimately lead to catastrophe.

- From Nazi Germany, we learned the horrors that ensue when a charismatic, megalomaniac leader manipulates the electorate's baser instincts by demonizing particular minorities who practice a different religion. Democracies can be transformed into police states given the right circumstances and the wrong politician.

- From World War II, we learned that free peoples can rally to overcome an existential threat to freedom. We also learned of the extraordinary destructive power of nuclear weapons, which are now fusion-based hydrogen bombs thousands of times stronger than the fission bombs dropped on Hiroshima and Nagasaki. Since World War II, governments have also figured out how to use guided missiles to travel across the globe to reach their targets.

- Major scientific breakthroughs have occurred. We have vaccines for smallpox and polio; Darwin showed us how species have evolved slowly over a billion years; Watson and Crick discovered that DNA contains the blueprint for life; modern scientists can modify DNA and RNA in living organisms, including humans; we invented trains, automobiles, planes and rockets that took man to the moon.

- Instead of spreading news on horseback like Paul

Revere, mankind invented the telegraph, the telephone, radio, TV, the Internet and Twitter.

- We now have the Internet, which promises the democratization of information, but also allows authoritarian governments to control information and allows Russia to attack democracies via fake news.

- We have been threatened by the rise of religious-based terrorism during the late 20th and early 21st centuries.

- Health care has become one of the largest sectors of Western economies, partially due to extraordinary advances in medicine, but also because modern civilization provides many of us our bare necessities (clean water, nutritious food, safe shelter) with much less effort than in 1787, which means we have the luxury of spending more time and money on realizing healthier and longer lives.

If the Founding Fathers had a crystal ball that showed them the changes listed above, they might have come up with significant changes to the American Constitution.

Therefore, society today is hugely different than in 1787. We should not pretend the constitutions supporting democracy today are sufficient by themselves to withstand modern threats. Those who believe in government of the people, by the people and for the people must work passionately to defend democracy and improve it using every available tool and technology so that freedoms are preserved and everyone benefits, not just the powerful few.

OBJECTIONS TO TRUE DEMOCRACY

Some people might say that the criteria for True Democracy listed at the beginning of this chapter are impossible to achieve in today's world. Among the common objections is the argument that legislation is too complex for the masses. Another is that the citizens are too busy and too disinterested to participate in the legislative process directly.

To this and other objections, I say keep reading because I will propose an incremental plan to make progress toward True Democracy a reality. It won't happen immediately, but instead gradually and steadily over the course of time.

The key ingredients will be mobilizing passions for democratic self-government (next chapter) and strategic use of technology (subsequent chapters).

5 Holy War

Throughout history, believers in democratic government have put forth incredible effort and sacrifice, the equivalent of a Holy War. People used to be willing to fight for the right to self-government and freedom from tyranny. A few examples:

- In the American Revolutionary War, the American colonists risked their lives to revolt against Great Britain and establish their own country where the people could govern themselves democratically (i.e., without a king). If the revolution had failed, the leaders would likely have been executed and the American people would probably have been punished with onerous taxes, military occupation and censorship of the press. Other colonies throughout the world followed the American lead and had their own revolutions of independence, such as the Latin

American and Caribbean wars for independence in the 19th century, [1]also risking life and livelihood in the process.

- The French people have taken to the streets many times to rebel against governments by the powerful few. There was the French Revolution of 1789, followed by rebellions in 1830, 1832, 1848 and 1871.

- In World War II, the democratic countries of the West partnered with the Soviet Union against Hitler's totalitarian Nazi regime, sacrificing over ten million soldiers to fight against the police state of Nazi Germany and the spread of fascism.

- In 1989, the Polish people rallied behind Lech Walesa and the Solidarity movement to free themselves from over 40 years of subjugation by the Soviet Union, known for its ruthless eradication of rebellions.

Today, most people in Western-style democracies from Western Europe to the Americas to Asia, are (sorry) soft, self-centered and spoiled. They generally wait passively for someone else to fight their battles. Most people's involvement in the democratic process ranges from nothing to limited and sporadic. For most, citizenship translates into occasional voting, or no voting at all; occasional small donations to candidates or causes; rare attendance at political events; and little effort to get informed.

A large part of this phenomenon is generational. Let's call the generation that fought in World War II the first generation. This generation understood just how fragile democratic society is, how much sacrifice is needed sometimes to fight back the threats and how vigilant we have to be to preserve democracy.

All of the major participants in World War II engaged in total war, where most aspects of society and industry were mobilized for the war effort. Nearly every able-bodied young adult male served in the military, with a substantial percentage facing the horrors of direct combat. Women generally stayed home to work in war factories. Industry was redirected toward war production. Between 1942 and 1945, the US alone produced 325,000 aircraft, 88,000 tanks, 1,400 major warships and 2,400,000 military trucks. [2] Scientists and mathematicians dropped their previous endeavors and worked on technology that would give their side an edge. Major technology advances included computers, nuclear energy, synthetic rubber, mass production of penicillin, radar, sonar, space missiles and jet engines, among many others. [3]

The generation that fought in World War II (which Tom Brokaw calls the "Greatest Generation" [4]) did not stop their efforts when the various armistices were signed; instead, the leading Western nations worked together on multiple supranational initiatives to prevent a repeat of the horrors of the two world wars, where an estimated combined 90 million people worldwide died in combat. [5] Here are some of the global institutions and programs established by the Greatest Generation in the wake of the second World War to prevent future wars, safeguard democracies, promote global free-enterprise and generally help all the people of the world:

- **United Nations** – an intergovernmental organization where all nations cooperate on global issues. Objectives include peacekeeping, security, human rights, economic development and humanitarian assistance. [6]

- **North Atlantic Treaty Organization (NATO)** – a collective defense treaty, along with shared military operations, between nations of North America (USA and Canada) and Europe (many nations), mostly as a military check against the Soviet Union. [7]

- **World Bank** – an international financial institution that provides loans to developing countries for capital programs. [8]

- **Marshall Plan** – a large-scale economic initiative by the USA to aid Western Europe to help rebuild Western European economies. [9]

- **International Court of Justice (World Court)** – the primary judicial branch of the United Nations in The Hague, Netherlands, which settles legal disputes among nations and provides advisory opinions on international legal questions. [10]

- **International Monetary Fund (IMF)** – an international organization that aids global monetary cooperation, financial stability, international trade, employment, economic growth and poverty reduction. [11]

- **General Agreement on Tariffs and Trade** – an international trade agreement to reduce tariffs and other trade barriers in order to promote global trade. [12]

- **Organization of American States** – organization of Western Hemisphere nations to promote regional solidarity and cooperation. [13]

- **Bretton Woods** – a system of monetary management rules for commercial and financial relations among the United States, Canada, Western Europe, Australia and Japan, which laid the groundwork for international monetary relations in the second half of the 20th century. [14]

Many of their children (second generation, the "Baby Boomers") had a much different perspective on the world than their parents. Instead of growing up in the Great Depression, the Baby Boomers of the West grew up in relative affluence with modern conveniences such as washing machines and automobiles. Many took democracy for granted, complaining about the "Establishment" as something that was bad, when in fact, the Establishment was the creation of the Greatest Generation to help preserve the democracies they had struggled so hard to make strong. The Baby Boomers did make amazing contributions, such as the Internet, mobile phones, mapping the human genome, voice recognition, voice synthesis and many passionate individuals who demanded that society live up to its ideals, fighting to eliminate racism, sexism, ageism and other forms of prejudice. But nevertheless many were either oblivious or took for granted the struggle to preserve self-government.

Now we are in the early stages of the third generation. Until now (early 2017), on average there is little appreciation for just how much of a fight was needed for democratic governments to prevail in both World War II and the Cold War. Preserving democracy is someone else's job. Instead, the third generation is often criticized for focusing too much of their attention on their smartphones (which is not necessarily a bad thing).

Government of the people, by the people, and for the people requires constant vigilance. As I explained in previous chapters, at this point in history, if democracy falls, it may never return because of the Big Brother technologies available to oppressive governments.

CALL TO ACTION

I call on passionate believers in government by the people, and passionate people who believe in Freedom, to become true democracy warriors. Invest significant time and effort. Make personal sacrifices for the common good. Even be willing to give up your life or livelihood in extraordinary circumstances if necessary to prevent tyranny enforced by a police state. Most significantly, people need to engage in the existing democratic process, such as voting, donating, making phone calls and sometimes running for elective office.

PASSION FOR THE DEMOCRATIC SYSTEM OVER YOUR OWN POLITICAL BELIEFS

In 2017, the West, including the USA, is divided ideologically, with strong passions on both sides. I am calling on people from both the Left and the Right to take a portion of their political activism and direct it towards a shared passion for a fair, honest democratic political system where the people control their own government, not the other way around; where people are not manipulated by false or misleading news sources; and where the government does not oppress its citizens via Big Brother techniques.

Many people will read the above paragraph and say, sure, motherhood and apple pie, but how specifically do we make progress. The rest of the book provides a prescription. Let's start with a set of common principles with which most who cherish democracy will agree.

UNIVERSAL VALUES AND BELIEFS

To avoid being subject to government by the powerful few, we have to agree on core principles – a shared set of common beliefs. Most good people today, regardless of religion or political affiliation, who desire to live under a fair and equitable democratic government will agree on the following universal values, which form the foundation for the ideas in this book.

- Love is better than hate.

- Peace is better than war. However, sometimes it is necessary to be strong and fight in order to preserve these universal values and beliefs. Fighting should be a last resort, and is only justified when no other viable approach is available.

- People should have basic freedoms, including life, liberty and the pursuit of happiness. Other basic freedoms include freedom of speech, religion, sexual orientation, political views and what activities you engage in, so long as your actions do not truly threaten the safety and well-being of others.

- Honesty and trustworthiness are better than dishonesty and untrustworthiness. In fact, honesty and trustworthiness are critical for a society to function efficiently. For example, if people can trust banks to hold their money, then people don't have to build secret safes on their property and don't have to hire guards to protect those safes. Trust brings economic efficiency, thereby freeing people so they have more time and energy for improving their lives and the lives of others.

- Kindness and compassion are better than meanness.

- Tolerance is better than intolerance. If someone else is different than what you are used to, such as different skin tone, dress, manner of speaking, sexual orientation, race, ethnicity, religion, political views, gender, disabilities or age, you should not be prejudiced against that person so long as that person does not truly threaten your safety or livelihood.

- People should balance self-interest with camaraderie and these universal values. Yes, everyone needs to take care of Number One (i.e., yourself), but only to the point that you don't harm others directly or indirectly, within the bounds of reason.

- The goal of government should be improving the general welfare of its citizens. Governments should not prioritize its own objectives or the objectives of the powerful few at the expense of citizens that have less power, particularly power based on money or arms.

- For a government to work well for its citizens, there

needs to be a set of laws that are policed and enforced by the government. However, the government should act fairly with all people, reflect the will of its citizens and allow people their basic freedoms. In particular, equal justice and opportunity for all.

- People should honor contracts and agreements, no matter if written or verbal.

- True science, where experts in a particular scientific domain follow the Scientific Method of hypothesis, test, publish methods and results, and allow other scientists to review and reproduce results, represents truth and fact for the things that science can explain.

- You cannot prevent people from being creative, which also means you cannot stop the inevitable advance of technology and knowledge. Because technology is now so powerful (e.g., nuclear bombs, guided missiles, satellites, planes, drones, genetic engineering, stock trading, etc.), it is necessary for governments to monitor and regulate technology, but only intervene when technology has the potential to harm people.

- People require the ability to socialize for multiple reasons. Most people cannot achieve happiness and fulfillment without some combination of family and friends. Socialization helps people learn from each other and helps correct destructive impulses and behaviors.

Socialization also helps diminish fear of others because we tend to be comfortable with the familiar.

- Today's world is dependent on people cooperating. Technology is so advanced and specialized that most people cannot be completely self-sufficient. Babies need to be guarded and nurtured by older people (usually parents). Most adults depend on governments for security, employers for jobs, stores for food and clothing and, these days, the Internet for information, commerce and social interaction. Most people require close relationships with other people (e.g., marriage, family and friendship) in order to realize happy and fulfilling lives.

- Trustworthy information and universal education is critical for a well-functioning society and for people to act in their own best interest. Falsehood, propaganda and bias from information sources are evil (usually emanating from someone who places self-interest above the common good) and serve to prevent people from acting in their own best interest.

- Mankind is now greatly interconnected and mutually interdependent. Therefore, there needs to be some level of world governance to prevent the self-serving actions of one country from harming other countries. Note that this comment primarily reflects the world as it exists today, where we have the U.N., the Geneva conventions, nuclear nonproliferation treaties, space treaties and trade agreements. World governance must be only as much as is needed and no more so that each country is free from potential world government oppression.

HOLY WAR FOR AND AGAINST WHAT?

We are fighting for:

- The universal values and beliefs listed in the previous section

- All people are created equal

- Each person has a set of inalienable rights, including life, liberty and the pursuit of happiness

- Government of the people, by the people and for the people

- Freedoms of speech, religion and peaceful assembly

- Freedom to live your life as you wish, so long as your actions do not harm or threaten others

- Rule of law applied equally

- Equal opportunity for all

- Equal power to all citizens to participate in government

- Equal access to information

- Honest and true information sources available to all people

- The pursuit of knowledge should not be restricted for ideological reasons

We are fighting against:

- Government controlled by the powerful few

- Prejudice and intolerance

- Authoritarian or oppressive governments

- Censorship

- False, misleading or manipulative information sources

HOLY WAR NEEDS TO BE A TOTAL WAR – ON ALL FRONTS

Authoritarian leaders establish full control over all aspects of society incrementally. Look at Nazi Germany for the blueprint:

- First, win a democratic election by appealing to citizens' nationalist fervor, demonizing one or more segments of society, stoking fear in the populace and promising strength against enemies. (Note that Hitler 's rise to power was somewhat circuitous. [15])

- Enlist partners who put selfish interests above national interest, particularly among political and industry leaders who see opportunities to profit by working with the strongman.

- Build perception of early success stories with your core

supporters, such as the appearance that new jobs are coming. It doesn't matter if the programs are actually good or not, you just need to solidify the support of your political base.

- Always appear strong. Bully those who lack the courage to fight back.

- Engage in some form of military engagement because a call to patriotism will broaden the number of people who support you.

- Have your surrogates get on the media to claim that anyone who is against the leader is unpatriotic.

- Use the fear of a threat or enemy to convince the country to give war powers to the leader.

- Gain control of the media slowly but surely until achieving full government control over information.

- Create a police state which includes invasive surveillance of all citizens.

As I mentioned earlier, it is much easier today to create Big Brother because of our dependence on the Internet for nearly all aspects of modern life.

So, how do you wage a Holy War against a rising authoritarian leader? First, the earlier the resistance, the better. (An ounce of protection is worth a pound of cure.) Second, the resistance has to be unwavering. Third, there needs to be brave, unselfish people willing to sacrifice their livelihoods and even their lives to fight against the slide towards tyranny. Fourth, the resistance needs to be a total, absolute war against the threat of tyranny and for the establishment and preservation of the democratic ideals which have been outlined in this chapter and the previous one.

Specifically:

- It is equally critical to raise donations from a large and diverse group of supporters to legitimize the movement as broad-based.

- Nearly all wars, military or political, cost huge amounts of money. If the tyrant has partnered with billionaires and large corporations, they have tremendous power to buy and coerce their way to absolute power. The resistance needs great money power, too, so it is essential to find rich people who believe in democratic ideals to join and help finance the movement.

- The movement will need powerful legal counsel to fight attempts to circumvent constitutional protections.

- Everyone in the movement should always be trustworthy and honest. If anyone in the movement deviates from these ideals, disavow and correct as soon as possible. The tyrant's team will put a spotlight on any comment that is untruthful, exaggerating its importance and distracting the media away from your other messages. (Trustworthiness is the focus of the next chapter.)

- Show determination and unity, such as public acts of protest. Media coverage of the dissent is crucial. If the media doesn't give positive coverage, the protests are either worth little or even counterproductive. Widely respected celebrities will help attract participation and media coverage, but manage their appearances carefully to minimize potential backfire. [16]

- Engage in the media via Op Eds and appearances on news programs. Note that news outlets are interested in things that are new. You may have to be clever about getting media attention while not compromising on trustworthiness.

- Engage in social media with the equivalent of a war plan. At the start, your movement will control certain territory in the world of social media (e.g., perhaps scientists' social media accounts), the tyrant will control other territory (e.g., perhaps the social media accounts of people with particular prejudices) and the rest will be neutral. Slowly but surely you need to develop and execute a social media invasion plan metaphorically similar to the Allied counterattacks against the Nazis in World War II, where invasions happened on the Eastern front, Africa, Italy, and Normandy. The war also took place in the air and at sea. The entire economies of the Allies were dedicated to the war; otherwise, the tyrant would not be defeated. The best engineers, scientists and mathematicians invented things to support the effort. Even with this total commitment, it still took nearly seven years to prevail. Fighting tyranny can be a huge effort, whether a physical war like WWII or a war of ideas.

- Produce popular art that depicts the danger of tyranny and the bravery of those people who are warriors for democracy. Some people do not pay close attention to politics, but they do see films, listen to music, go to shows and laugh at animated GIFs.

- Let no instance of falsehood and propaganda go unchallenged.

- Stay as pure as possible in the commitment to shared democratic ideals as outlined in this book. Avoid mixing in partisan issues because the tyrant's team will talk about the partisan comments to divert public attention away from the threat to democracy and freedom.

- Enlist support from both the Left and the Right to have credibility that the movement is about saving democracy, not promoting a partisan agenda.

- Donate and get involved in existing nonpartisan efforts whose mission is to preserve democracy.

- Support and donate to a free and open media.

- Support candidates across the nation who have come out publicly against the tyrant for democratic reasons, regardless of political views.

- Make sure to appeal to young people. Young people can influence older people by their strong convictions and determination. Furthermore, young people will be the future warriors for democracy.

6 Prioritizing Trustworthiness

TRUST MAKES OUR LIVES MORE EFFICIENT

Our trust in someone or something is our belief in the likelihood that a desired outcome will actually happen. For example, we trust that the Earth will continue to rotate around the sun, and we trust our cell phones to accurately give us the date and time. On the human side, even if we drive defensively, we trust that drivers stopped at a red light will wait for their light to turn green before entering the intersection. In commerce, we trust Starbucks to deliver a particular beverage quality and ambience no matter where in the world we find a store. In the West, we trust the government in various ways even if we are naturally cynical, such as trusting the fire department to come in case of fire.

In the age of the Internet and social media, we trust people we don't know all of the time. When we are deciding on which restaurant to go for dinner, we often rely on restaurant reviews written by unknown people. When we bid on something at an auction site, we look at seller ratings from people we don't know to decide whether the promise of a bargain is worth the chance the seller is dishonest. When we need to learn about an unfamiliar topic, we usually feel we can trust the information we find in the crowd-sourced online encyclopedia Wikipedia, particularly for topics without ideological controversy.

Without trust, life would be much less convenient and more stressful. Suppose we could not trust that interstate highways are safely maintained – e.g., suppose those highways were often full of potholes and various forms of metal debris. Then, driving would be highly stressful and traffic would slow to a crawl. Fortunately, in reality, the government is highly trustworthy in maintaining the interstates, so we feel confident as we drive fast.

On the world stage, many countries in the West have no military or an inadequate one because they trust the USA to protect them (and uphold America's traditional ideals in the process).

IMPERFECTIONS WITH TRUST IN SOCIETY TODAY

People take shortcuts when deciding whom or what to trust. These shortcuts cause mistakes.

We trust the familiar more than the unfamiliar. This explains brand loyalty – why we always buy the same brand of underwear or we go to movies with actors we know. It is also why some people fear people with different clothing, language, hair, skin color or religion. Foreign exchange programs for high school students tend to increase trust across cultures partly because they increase familiarity.

We rely on indirect trust, even if it is wrong. Suppose our friend Tom seems to know everything from how to do home repair to the family history of everyone in town. We believe Tom is a trustworthy source of information because no one else we know comes close to his level of knowledge on those topics, and Tom always sounds so authoritative. Tom recently read a book recommended by his friend extolling the virtues of cabbage juice. We trust Tom and therefore start drinking lots of cabbage juice (at least until we start feeling sick).

High-technology marketing gurus describe this indirect string of information sources as the word-of-mouth influencing pyramid, first articulated by Regis McKenna.[1] Here is a picture adapted with permission from a personal branding book [2] that illustrates the influencing pyramid in action when someone who needs surgery tries to find the best surgeon.

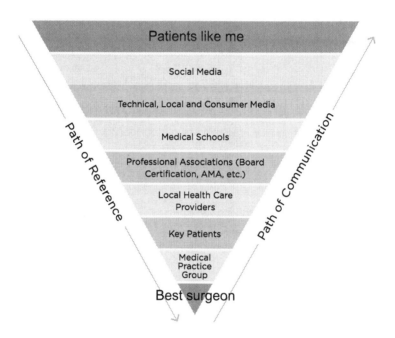

The patient finds the surgeon by checking social media, where people with more knowledge than the patient make a recommendation. But where do the people on social media get their information? From people further down the pyramid. The pyramid narrows because fewer and fewer people have expert knowledge.

The same word-of-mouth information flow happens in the world of politics. People who do not follow politics closely will generally form opinions based on what they hear from people they trust who seem to have more expertise. Perhaps you trust the political information from cabbage-juice Tom!

There is also the halo effect, [3] where we trust a particular politician (e.g., Obama or Trump) completely because their rhetoric matches our beliefs. Thus, many liberals trusted Obama when he said, if you like your current health-care policy, you can keep it. Similarly, if you are conservative, you might truly believe Mexico will pay for that wall.

Therefore, we take shortcuts with trust that sometimes results in imperfect results.

THERE ARE MANY CERTIFIED TRUSTWORTHY PEOPLE AROUND US

Therefore, trust is both crucial and, in many cases, error-prone; however, there are countless examples in modern life where we are able to trust others with a very high probability that the trusted person or organization will deliver the results we expect:

- Gallup polling shows that we trust nurses, pharmacists and medical doctors

- We trust engineers to design safe bridges, roads and airplanes
- We trust our judges, juries and court workers to follow court procedures properly
- We trust our fire services, police, and EMTs to help us in emergencies (exception: in America, the Black Lives Matter [4] movement shows that not everyone trusts the police)
- We trust religious leaders to honor their faith and religious vows
- Generals trust that their soldiers will follow all orders to the best of their abilities
- In many countries, we trust special financial services professionals, called fiduciaries, to always act honestly with only the client's best interests in mind
- We trust notary publics to faithfully witness signatures on documents

The commonality with all of the above:

- They are highly trained in their job
- They have been indoctrinated about their duty and/or have taken oaths
- They have a lot to lose both professionally and personally if they deviate from their duty/ trustworthiness

Note that our trust for nurses, firemen, fiduciaries, etc. only applies to specific areas and not to everything in life. For example, we trust doctors with our medical needs, and we trust firemen to put out fires, but we wouldn't trust either to design a passenger airplane. Therefore:

- Trust applies only to particular areas of expertise and particular situations

RATING SERVICES HELP DETERMINE TRUSTWORTHY VENDORS AND PRODUCTS

Online services allow people to rate and post comments on vendors, products and services. These sites help consumers to know whom and what to trust. If we are traveling and looking for a hotel or restaurant, rating sites will help. If we are looking for a good book, there are book review sites. Today, countless services rate various categories of products.

Users often use stars (e.g., one to four or five) to rate the product. Sometimes the ratings site then averages the ratings to come up with a composite rating, such 2.3 (not good) or 4.9 (excellent) for a one to five scale.

The rating services are a great tool for consumers to find vendors or products with a high expectation of delivering the desired results. However, most rating services have obvious shortcomings:

- Unscrupulous reviewers – e.g., the vendor might have employees and friends write favorable reviews

- Unqualified reviewers – an ignoramus might give a bad review to a great high-end restaurant because he didn't appreciate the formal atmosphere and high prices

- Reviewers with a different point of view – a restaurant reviewer of a noisy restaurant might not care about the volume, but perhaps the noise would be unbearable to you because of a hearing aid

- Often, a product will have too few or no reviews for the reader to feel confident in the composite rating

TRUSTWORTHY INFORMATION SOURCES – GOVERNMENT AND POLITICS

Therefore, there are many examples of individuals who are trustworthy within their domain of expertise. Do we have any similarly trusted professionals in the media who we can rely on for accurate and complete information about government and politics?

The answer is yes, but with major caveats. Pew Research did a study of major news organizations in America [5] and found that there was one organization that was generally trusted by both ideological liberals and conservatives (The Wall Street Journal) and one which is trusted by most and untrusted by none (BBC). Some news organizations are generally trusted by everyone except strong conservatives

(The Economist, ABC, USA Today and Google News), and several are close behind (CNN, NPR, Bloomberg, NBC and CBS). Fox is trusted by conservatives and people of mixed ideology but distrusted by liberals. Note: the Associated Press was not in the survey, but it is generally respected as nonpartisan and professional.

One of the big issues with the 2016 and 2017 elections in the USA and Europe is fake news, much of which was sponsored by Russia, where false articles influence unsuspecting voters to cast their ballots in a way that serves Russia's interests. The American intelligence services concluded that Russian goals were to undermine Western democracies and, in particular in the US, help Trump defeat Clinton. [6] Many in the UK believe Russia influenced the Brexit vote using tactics that included and went beyond fake news. [7] Clearly, democracy will fail if the voters unwittingly see false information in the media.

To fight against fake news, Facebook has recently partnered with several nonpartisan fact-checking organizations (initially, with Snopes, Politifact, ABC News and FactCheck.org) to flag fake news. [8]

Note that this only addresses completely bogus stories. It doesn't address heavily biased articles with falsehoods or misleading information.

Another shortcoming with existing news sources in the

West is that many voters purposefully choose to follow news outlets that cater to their preconceived ideology. Friends on Facebook share biased articles with each other, creating echo chambers for the Left and the Right, thereby increasing political divisions. Many people are more interested in reinforcing their ideology rather than trying to understand the points of view of the other side. (Usually the other side's point of view is equally valid, and usually there is a consensus common ground that can be found if only people would tone down their emotions.) The Wall Street Journal created an online tool to show the echo chamber effect. [9]

Another big obstacle is partisanship, where a political party cares more about winning the next election than the welfare of its citizens. One classic example cited by American Democrats was when leading Republicans publicly stated during Barack Obama's first term that they had the specific goal of obstructing him so he would appear to have a failed presidency and therefore lose his bid for reelection. [10] Note that Republicans counter this claim by saying it is important to look at exactly what they said [11] and how the Democrats steamrolled Obamacare through Congress without a single Republican vote. [12]

CAN WE DO BETTER?

In the above sections, I argued that society depends on trust; there are countless examples of trust working effectively; there are many imperfections; most of the information sources on government and politics are distrusted by large blocks of voters; there are major problems with fake news; and voters are more interested in reading articles that support their ideology than in listening to others and potentially learning the truth.

Can we make things better? I believe so – if we take advantage of most people's innate desire to be good in combination with leveraging technology.

PROPOSAL: TRUSTWORTHINESS INTERNET IDENTITIES

I propose a global, crowd-sourced trustworthiness Internet service that collects trustworthiness reviews on people and organizations who provide information on government and politics. The Internet service would:

- Collect trustworthiness reviews and rating scores from the public and store them in the cloud with full transparency on every aspect of its operations

- Compute two numeric values for each Internet ID (person or organization): an average trustworthiness rating and a confidence value on that rating

- Generate a small icon that conveys at a glance the trustworthiness of a particular individual or organization

- Work with the media and news aggregators to show the trustworthiness icon next to the byline of news articles so that readers can see at a glance the trustworthiness of the author (person or organization)

- Promote the service so that its use is widespread, and thereby pressure government, politicians, the media and pundits to be more honest in their communications

In the early stages, before the movement and its umbrella organization have achieved critical mass, the organization will provide browser extensions, such as a Google Chrome extension, so early adopters can start using the icon before the big aggregators and media companies display the icon by default.

The following sections provide detail.

FOCUS: INFORMATION SOURCES ON GOVERNMENT AND POLITICS

We need to have a clear focus both on whose trustworthiness we need to measure and in what domain we focus.

It is impractical to attempt to measure the trustworthiness of every person and organization in the world; therefore, we narrow the spotlight onto people and organizations (Internet IDs) that are information providers on government and politics. We start with Internet IDs with the largest following or greatest influence. It is fine if the choices of whom to evaluate first are imperfect because as the service grows, the breadth and depth of coverage will grow until most important Internet IDs have trustworthiness reviews submitted by people who are both highly competent at trustworthiness reviews (there will be training programs and judgments on the trustworthiness judges) and highly trustworthy (each judge will have his own trustworthiness score).

It is imprecise and impractical to attempt to measure the trustworthiness of an individual across all aspects of their lives. A given person will have a professional life, a community life, a social life, a family life and a spiritual life. Perhaps the person is extremely honest with his friends and family, but when talking politics, he spreads falsehoods. For our purposes, we only care about:

- Communications about government and politics
- Communications that are posted on the Internet (with a permanent URL) and are verifiably authentic, preferably posted by the person or organization itself

Among the things that will be evaluated:

- Articles posted on the Web, including opinion pieces and blogs
- Books

- Audio and video posted on the Web
- Publicly available social media posts, including tweets

ADMINISTERED BY A NONPROFIT THAT IS RUN AS A TRUE DEMOCRACY

We need a formal organization to manage and administer the overall effort to bring true democracy to the world, including the first initiative outlined in this chapter – Trustworthy Internet Identities. Let's call the organization Democracy Guardians (DG).

Because DG is all about trustworthiness and true democracy:

- It will be a nonprofit – it can't have even the hint of financial conflict of interest
- It will be operated as a true democracy – it will eat its own dog food
- The board of directors will be voted on by the members, using weighted votes where the votes of people with the highest trustworthiness scores will count more than people with low scores
- The board will choose an executive team, which in turn will hire employees
- Anyone in the world can become a member, but note that a person's influence on DG decisions will depend

on the person's trustworthiness score, which will initially be the equivalent of zero

- Members can build a trustworthiness score by either posting about government and politics (and thereby getting judged by others) or by participating in DG activities such as taking training courses and then submitting trustworthiness judgments on others (all judgments will be reviewed by more senior members of DG)

- DG will be open and transparent in everything – every bit of communication among DG board and staff will be posted on the Web, every vote will be public, every line of computer code will be public open source except encryption keys and other administrative secrets

INTERNET IDS

An Internet identity represents an actual person or organization that has a presence on the Internet in the form of material such as articles, blog posts, audio, video or social media posts that capture that person's statements and opinions about government and politics.

Examples of Internet IDs are politicians, spokespersons, news organizations, pundits, experts in particular domains and business leaders. Even many normal people without any celebrity will have Internet IDs, sometimes because that person is a member of DG and every member must have an Internet ID.

Basically, anyone who is in the DG cloud database (usually, because they are members of DG or their trustworthiness is being judged by some member of DG) will get an Internet ID. Each person or organization with an Internet ID will have a profile that contains the following information:

- Name(s) by which the person or organization is known, including nicknames

- Public email, twitter handles, other public social media IDs, blogs, websites and any other Internet IDs. LinkedIn will be valuable in certain countries.

- Biographical info, preferably with details such as near ancestors, birth, schooling, professional life and for what the subject is most well-known, if anything

DG will pursue Web search technology that can crawl through the Web and build a database of Twitter handles, email addresses, Facebook pages, website URLs and many other things that might represent a person or organization. Then, when it's time to create a new profile, the DG app or website will auto fill the fields in the profiles to speed the process of filling out the profile. DG members would manually review and correct.

A by-product of the above technologies will be a world-class database of Internet identities (people and organizations) which will allow for future technology initiatives and revenue generation.

DG DEFINITION OF TRUSTWORTHINESS

Simply put, trustworthiness is the ability to be relied on as honest or truthful.

Trustworthiness also can be defined as being worthy of trust, which I earlier defined as our belief in the likelihood that a desired outcome will actually happen. For DG, the desired outcome is true and complete information about government and politics.

Said another way, for DG, a trustworthy person or organization reliably reports factual information based on verifiable evidence and provides unbiased interpretation of that information such that the people can be fully informed, which will allow them to participate in their own governance without ideological manipulation.

JUDGMENTS

A "judgment" is when a DG member submits an evaluation of the trustworthiness of a person or organization.

Let's call the person submitting a judgment the "judge"

and the Internet identity who is being judged the "subject".

The judge starts by running the DG mobile app or going to the DG website in a web browser. To create a new judgment, the user clicks on the "Add judgment" button.

If the judge is not currently logged in, a login/register screen will appear. Note that only registered users can submit judgments. Login and registration will be conventional, except that registration will require that the user create or update the information in his/her profile.

The user will now see the initial screen for the Add Judgment feature. The user experience will be a series of sequential steps (a wizard UX with Next buttons on each step with alternative ability to jump to any step at any time). On mobile devices each step would be a separate screen:

- The first step will be **the Add Judgment welcome screen.** If this is the first time the user has created a judgment, then **training material** will show, including video(s). The training material will be based on the user's current DG "level". Each member starts at level one and can get promoted to higher levels based on completion of training material and approval by another member who is at a higher level. The training material will explain the importance of being careful, thorough and unbiased, and how your judgment will be reviewed by someone with a higher DG level, who will judge your judgment as a combination of scoring your effort and mentoring you in how to create the best possible judgments.

- Then, **the judge identifies the subject** by supplying various ways to identify the subject, such as name, email, Twitter handle, etc. If the DG app can guess who the subject is, the app will attempt to autofill information about the subject; otherwise, the judge will have to create the subject's profile from scratch. The judge should verify and correct any autofilled information to make sure that the subject's profile is complete and correct.

- Then, **the judge enters multiple pieces of evidence** that best illuminate the subject's trustworthiness. Most of the evidence will be in the form of URLs, but in some cases will be textual descriptions if a suitable URL cannot be found. The DG server will attempt to retrieve and verify the URL and then save a snapshot in case the URL might deliver different data in the future.

- Then, the judge will choose a **trustworthiness score** (1-9) for the subject, along with a textual justification for the score.

- Then, the judge will choose a **confidence score** (1-9) where the judge provides his own confidence about how accurate his judgment is, along with a textual justification for the score.

- Then, the **review step** will appear where the judge will see a summary of his judgment, along with any errors and warnings about the judgment that is about to be submitted. The judge can either navigate back to modify the data or press the **Submit Judgment** to upload his judgment.

- Finally, the **Thank you** step where some text appears that says the subject will get the opportunity to review and give feedback. The text will also note that someone at a higher level will review the judgment before the judgment will be added as an approved judgment, possibly changing content, the trustworthiness score and confidence score.

Whenever a judgment has been submitted or modified, the subject will be sent a notification (e.g., an email). The subject will have full control over the subject's portion of his/her profile and can submit feedback on any judgments on his/her trustworthiness.

Note that there is no anonymity in this process. People have to have the courage to stand up publicly for truth and accuracy so that we can increase the trustworthiness of information on government and politics, and thereby improve democracy such that it really is government of the people, by the people and for the people.

After a new judgment or revised judgment is approved, notifications will be sent to the subject, judge and any DG members who have registered for notifications.

MEMBER LEVELS

Each DG member will be at a particular level. New members start at level one. To get promoted to the next level, a member must complete a list of tasks (e.g., judgments) with a higher level member flagging the tasks as demonstrating particular learned skills (e.g., careful review of autofill entries) and must complete the training exercises for the next level.

The decision to promote a member to a higher level will be done automatically by DG software. The human angle comes in when higher level members review the contributions (e.g., judgments).

JUDGMENT GUIDELINES

To maximize consistency between judgments created by different people, DG will develop training materials that members must take in order to be promoted to the next higher level. These training materials will explain new concepts in how to judge trustworthiness properly, with test questions that verify that the user does indeed understand the new concepts. Other test questions will test previously learned concepts from lower levels (if any) to help ensure members still remember.

Here is a preliminary list of judgment guidelines:

Entry level:

- Trustworthiness defined (see "DG definition of trustworthiness" section above)

- Introducing judgments (see "Judgments" section above)

- DG vows (see the "Vows" section below)

- Fundamental judgment concepts:

- ○ Most people are honest most of the time. Just being honest most of the time is normal and should not be justification for giving someone a high trustworthiness score.

  ○ Being a good person or likeable or popular should have no effect on someone's trustworthiness score.

  ○ What actually counts in a positive way is evidence of material (written, audio, video, etc.) from the subject demonstrating commitment to the complete truth backed by verifiable evidence without bias, omissions and distortions, and without attempt to manipulate the opinions of others for ideological or self-serving reasons.

- ◦ Any deviations from trustworthiness must be weighted heavily negatively towards the subject's trustworthiness score. Note: if a subject deviates from trustworthiness in one particular case, but quickly and effectively fixes the deviation, then the judge should consider either giving the subject a pass or a smaller negative weight on the deviation.

Intermediate:

- Deeper training on judgments
- Training on how to review judgments submitted by lower level members

Advanced (Administrator level):

- Advanced members are required to have very high trustworthiness scores, high competence and the ability to serve effectively as a DG organization leader
- Advanced members will function as ultimate judges when difficult situations arise
- They will review the work of lower level members, particularly intermediate members

VOWS

Most humans are wired to be good. For those people, a promise carries importance – it represents a lightweight contract between two people.

A vow, or oath, is a more serious promise, in fact a contract, and a solemn vow takes precedence over most things in life.

Vows are a linchpin for a well-functioning society. We give vows when we marry, assume public office, give testimony in court, enter medical school (the Hippocratic oath), join the priesthood and join the military.

When becoming a member of Democracy Guardians, you must also make vows. When engaged in DG activities, DG members vow:

- to always be honest
- to tell the whole truth and nothing but the truth to the best of your ability
- to act out of unselfish love of life and others
- to work towards better trust relationships between the people and organizations of the world
- to commit absolutely to increasing the collective well-being of mankind

These simple vows provide DG a foundation of strength because they are based on true love for humanity; willingness to collaborate and compromise, to both give and receive; and unsurpassed zealousness and determination to achieve selflessness and goodness.

These vows will appear when a new user registers to become a DG member, and are formally agreed to when the user clicks to accept the DG member's agreement. Whenever a member performs a significant act within DG, such as adding a new judgment, the user interface will remind them of their vows.

Vows will be enforced by the community via trustworthiness judgments. If someone is discovered having betrayed his vows, his trustworthiness score will suffer.

Note that these vows only apply when engaged in DG activities, such as when working on a judgment. It is not necessary to honor the vows when not engaged in DG activities.

OVERALL TRUSTWORTHINESS SCORE: WEIGHTED

DG trustworthiness scores on Internet identities are weighted by two things:

- A confidence value that the judge provides when

submitting a judgment (see the earlier section titled "Judgments")

- The trustworthiness score of the judgment reviewer

Remember that each judgment will be reviewed by a higher level DG member. The subject of the judgment will have an opportunity to review, too, if the subject so desires.

When computing the overall trustworthiness score for an Internet identity, DG algorithms will weight high confidence judgments more than low confidence judgements and will weight judgments from people with high trustworthiness scores more than judgments from less trustworthy people. Initial algorithms might use a simple fractional multiplier approach for the weighting factors, but over time mathematicians and social scientists might come up with improved mathematical approaches.

Therefore, DG software algorithms will calculate a consensus judgment score that takes into account the various confidence and DG scores of the judges and reviewers, which will usually produce a consensus opinion based on conclusions from informed, trustworthy people. Note that this approach contains a good deal of subjective opinion, so the results will not be precise. Nevertheless, they will tend to show which information sources are reliable and which are not, with written documentation to back up the judgment. Furthermore, these scores will motivate information providers to be trustworthy to avoid public rebuke.

HOW THE SYSTEM WILL SELF-PROTECT AGAINST ABUSE

The design of the trustworthiness platform outlined above will be protected against attempts to commandeer, abuse or corrupt. It is critical that the founding members are considered good and trustworthy with their management of DG. Thus, the founding members need to have a diverse but representative set of philosophies on government and politics, with a balance between Left and Right. But even more important is a convincing history of being able to always put the True Democracy ideals described in this book ahead of their own political views.

But even if the founding members have some imperfect participants, the system will discover and purge leaders who are not performing as required. Other leaders and other members will be obligated by their vows to expose the problematic people in positions of power and appropriate reassignments will take place.

The trustworthiness platform has protections against an overwhelming onslaught of new members who might want to take over the platform by attempting to outvote the true members. As stated earlier, new members start off with the equivalent of zero trustworthiness and can only gain real voting power by contributions that are evaluated by higher level members. An unusually large number of new members will be noticed and the existing members will be on guard.

Thus, the culture of DG will start with trustworthiness and absolute fealty to vows at its very core. Strong culture can benefit both the organization and the people in the organization. [13]

THE ICON

All of the above work will be visible to the world in the form of a tiny icon (as small as 16px square).

Because this chapter is long and dense, I will repeat the five bullets first listed in "Trustworthy Internet Identities" above that summarize this chapter:

- Collect trustworthiness reviews and rating scores from the public and store them in the cloud with full transparency on every aspect of its operations

- Compute two numeric values for each Internet ID (person or organization): an average trustworthiness rating and a confidence value on that rating

- Generate a small icon that conveys at a glance the trustworthiness of a particular individual or organization

- Work with the media to show the trustworthiness icon

next to the byline of news articles so that readers can see at a glance the trustworthiness of the author (person or organization)

- Promote the service so that its use is widespread, and thereby pressure government, politicians, the media and pundits to be more honest in their communications

The instructions to the icon designer:

- The icon will be server-generated dynamically, with different icons generated for each different instance

- The icon should have one visual aspect that is recognizable as the DG trustworthiness symbol

- The icon should have one visual aspect that conveys a range of trustworthiness values, such as a color gradient from brown (extremely untrustworthy) to green (extremely trustworthy)

- The icon should have one visual aspect that conveys a range of confidence values, such as a color gradient from black (extremely unconfident) to white (extremely confident)

- The icon should be scalable from 16px square to any larger size and be renderable on modern Web browsers

7 Towards True Democracy

This chapter provides more detail on Democracy Guardians (DG), which was introduced in the previous chapter. It includes possible future initiatives beyond the trustworthiness initiative described earlier.

AN INNOVATIVE NONPROFIT THAT PROMOTES GOVERNMENT OF THE PEOPLE, FOR THE PEOPLE AND BY THE PEOPLE

DG is an nonprofit organization that embraces all possible tools, such as technology, media and entertainment, to help move the world towards true democracy where governments are truly of the people, by the people and for the people. DG's mission is to channel the passions of people who share a vision for self-government in order to strengthen democratic institutions, and thereby promote governments that serve the interests of all of the people, not just the powerful few.

Initially, DG will focus on increasing the trustworthiness of information sources on government and politics (see previous chapter), thereby increasing public pressure for truth from media outlets, elected politicians, government administrators and other organizations and individuals who are in positions of power. This will lessen the ability of bad actors from using falsehoods to drive hate and violence, and give the citizens more influence on people in power. A by-product will be a world-class database of Internet identities (people and organizations) which will allow for future technology initiatives and revenue generation.

DG is nonpartisan, including which form of government is the most preferred. Therefore, even though DG will work to make existing constitutional, democratic governments more effective as a primary mission, DG will be compatible with any form of government, including benevolent dictatorships. Bottom-line: DG wants governments to meet their citizens' needs. It is not designed to promote a single approach.

DG will pursue strength in many areas, including financial, legal, technology, innovation and marketing. DG's strength will also come from its many trust relationships with people and organizations, its positive reputation and goodwill accumulated over time.

The DG movement will use a wide variety of innovative

approaches and technologies to build greater power that will allow it to have a significant positive influence on society. Innovation will play a major role. DG will accomplish its goals in part by taking full advantage of various techniques and technologies that are controlled today by proprietary interests (e.g., for-profit companies own most Internet and social media platforms, and much of the news originates from special interests such as political parties). It is expected that DG will invent new approaches and technologies to achieve its goals.

If there is strong consensus among DG members that some amount of extra effort and sacrifice is necessary and desirable to counteract a threat, then DG will leverage its power to counter that threat. DG needs to be both well-meaning and strong.

It is incumbent on all members that the DG brand represents goodness and is no threat to existing benign or neutral interests. Therefore, a key operational requirement is that DG has a generally positive reputation to minimize the amount of friction from society. In the USA, the goal is approximately proportional membership across the American political spectrum.

For Western democracies, DG will generally support values that align with both the Left and Right, such as equality, fairness, freedom, free enterprise, individual initiative, free markets, safety, family and general well-being. In the West there is a strong consensus around these values and there is strong evidence that there is a good opportunity for people to be healthy, happy and fulfilled when society embraces these values. But some less democratic government might also give its citizens the same opportunities. For example, people seem reasonably well off in the Principality of Monaco. Even for autocratic governments, there might be a role for DG to incrementally move the government towards serving its citizens better simply by helping government and citizens jointly participate in DG. However, DG will have difficulty penetrating authoritarian governments that oppress their citizens via total control over information and offer few freedoms.

DG is non-opinionated about religion. DG will partner with religious people and organizations when goals align and DG does not have to compromise on its core values. It is expected that DG will have members who belong to most major religions because DG values and goals are largely in alignment.

DG believes in true science, where hypotheses are proven by facts or theory backed by compelling verifiable scientific evidence and experimentation. For example, DG members have a consensus that the Earth revolves around the Sun, not the other way around, partly because mankind could not have successfully sent spacecraft around the solar system if the scientific theories were wrong.

When engaged in DG activities, DG members vow: to act out of unselfish love of life and others; to work towards better trust relationships between the people and organizations of the world; and to commit absolutely to increasing the well-being of mankind. These simple vows provide DG a foundation of strength because they are based on true love for humanity; willingness to collaborate and compromise, to both give and receive; and unsurpassed zealousness and determination to achieve selflessness and goodness.

DG has noble goals and puts high expectations on participants, but only requires these good behaviors when participating in DG activities.

Participation in DG activities will be fun and joyful, and often will lead to both personal and professional growth.

DG believes people should live rich and fulfilling lives, so DG generally regards fun, pleasure, comfort, security, camaraderie, spirituality, style, music, dance and all of the arts as beneficial and sometimes essential. DG believes in individuality, freedom and self-expression because humans are naturally creative, and this creativity will lead to improvements in people's lives.

BOOTSTRAPPING AND GROWING THE ORGANIZATION

Here are the phases:

- **Phase 1: Early prototyping and initial fund-raising**

  - **Hire short-term, (mostly) part-time, inexpensive contractors (or volunteers) to build a live prototype of the trustworthiness initiative.** It is expected that about half of the effort will involve exploring the most effective ways of collecting data and writing up the trustworthiness judgments described in the previous chapter. One key question is how best to discover deviations from total truthfulness – perhaps often it will be most efficient to contact journalists familiar with the subject to accelerate the research. Probably only a small percentage of the ultimate trustworthiness software system will be written at this time as the major objective is learning, not a finished product. DG will look for contractors with creativity and writing skills because it will be important to capture what is learned so that it can be transformed into self-learning training materials for the future when DG scales up to a large number of members who are submitting trustworthiness judgments. Much of the work in the prototypes will likely have to be redone in the future. It is expected that there will be at least two prototypes developed, each taking a few months.

- **Fund-raising efforts will start immediately.** For the public at large, there will be a Donate button on the DG website. The author and early enthusiasts will ask for donations from people in their networks. All net proceeds from this book will go to DG. The early funds will go towards start-up expenses, website hosting and the contractors working on the prototypes.

- **Start recruiting an initial board of directors and founding chairman**, who would take over the fund-raising and planning process for the next phase.

- **Complete all of the formal requirements for a proper nonprofit.**

- **Phase 2: DG starts formal operations**

  - The board of directors will develop an initial set of bylaws and various legal documents, such as a Membership Agreement.

  - The board of directors will hire a CEO and help the CEO recruit the initial employees.

  - Develop the initial release of the trustworthiness platform.

  - Find a segment of the news universe that DG can

cover mostly with trustworthiness judgments. By focusing on one segment, DG can generate critical mass within a smaller universe at first. Other segments will be added over time.

- ◦ Sign up content aggregators to start displaying the trustworthiness icon next to article bylines.

- **Phase 3++: Later phases**

  - ◦ The employees and members decide how DG is managed, including voting to choose the board of directors. The nonprofit runs as a True Democracy, trying out some of the long-term technology initiatives outlined later in this chapter.

JOINING AND COMMITTING: EASY

Membership in DG will be easy – just register on the DG website, which involves reading and accepting the Membership Agreement.

Each person can only join once and must register using the person's true name and identity.

The key requirement from the Agreement is that, whenever participating in DG activities, you promise to always act under the general notions of goodness listed in the Agreement. This obligation only applies to DG activities, not to your life outside of DG. As a consequence, if you join DG but never participate, then there was never a time when you were obligated to act with goodness.

Acting with goodness requires no effort; in fact, it usually works best when you eliminate effort. Just relax, release all selfishness and let your inherent goodness come out. In psychological terms, trust your conscience.

PARTICIPATION: FUN AND ENTERTAINING (GAMING USER INTERFACE)

Most participation in DG activities will involve people using DG's website and apps voluntarily, without payments or fees, similar to Wikipedia. To make participation fun for all, particularly young people, most user interfaces will have elements of gaming.

Upon first joining, you will be at level one. As you participate and contribute, you are evaluated and scored. As your score and other criteria grow, you will advance to higher levels, each with small but significant additional requirements on the given user. Examples of additional requirements include acquisition of particular skills, acquisition of knowledge and completion of DG work assignments, such as submitting judgments on other Internet identities.

Scores will be based partially on how the other DG members judge your contributions.

PARTNERSHIP WITH OTHER ORGANIZATIONS WITH OVERLAPPING GOALS OR ACTIVITIES

DG will welcome and often pursue collaboration with other organizations, with the requirement that all such collaboration aligns with DG's mission, objectives and principles. In particular, DG will want other organizations to embrace DG's trustworthiness platform because that will increase the overall level of trust in society.

FINANCES

DG will be serious about financial management and vigilant about financial strength, which will provide defense against potential attacks by selfish or destructive forces:

- DG will have sophisticated fund-raising efforts
- DG will charge nominal fees to other organizations for use of its technologies:

- ○ There will be fees for high-volume usage of DG's trustworthiness APIs

  ○ There will be license royalties for use of some DG technologies by certain types of users

  ○ ■ Trustworthy nonprofits would get the lowest possible fees, hopefully most times free or at cost

- Other organizations would be subject to higher fees, though still reasonable

- Note that the same technologies that will work for crowd-sourced trustworthiness scores can be applied to other attributes, such as knowledge, skills, opinions, likes and reviews that lend themselves to commercialization. These areas might be a good opportunity for DG revenue generation, particularly if DG has patents around some of its key technologies.

- DG members who reach high trustworthiness scores will often be able to monetize their reputation for being a trustworthy source of information on government and politics. For example, a lawyer who has a high trustworthiness score might have a stronger brand in the marketplace due to that score. DG members who also have expertise in particular areas will sometimes be in demand for paid speaking, consulting, contract work or media appearances, or even just a lucrative position in the world of commerce. When DG members receive payment for activities somehow due partly to DG scores, then DG asks that member to give a (usually small) fraction of the payment to DG. This would be done on an honor system as a form of give back.

- All financial transactions will be instantly available to the public the moment they happen.

LEGAL

DG will be a properly registered nonprofit organization. Due to its focus on innovation, it is likely that DG will have some intellectual property. In general, DG will look to monetize its IP when used by for-profit entities, but at low-pain terms and conditions. Anyone who uses any DG IP will have to agree to a fairly standard user agreement.

POSSIBLE LONG-TERM INITIATIVES

If the initial phases of DG are successful, the DG management team may decide to pursue other major initiatives that would further the goals of more trustworthy information that leads to better governance and better lives, and progress towards true democracy as defined in this book. Here are some possibilities:

- **Educational initiatives** that teach people how to be a successful DG activist. Additionally, there will be educational programs that help individuals develop particular skills which result in benefit either to society or to the given individual. Other possibilities are programs that target young people, such as summer camps and internships where the person has fun, develops skills, makes contributions and learns about civics.

- **Evangelism initiatives** that reach out to and engage with as broad of a spectrum of citizens as possible, being sure to prioritize engagement with people most likely to be ignorant or distrustful of DG. It will be important that DG prioritize efforts to avoid being exclusive, elitist or insular.

- **A media presence** that helps the movement pursue its goals, possibly including:

  ○ One or more TV stations on cable, Internet, radio and other media channels

  ○ Major state-of-the-art social media efforts

  ○ It is likely that DG will want to create original content

- **Technology initiatives that help advance the movement's goals.** One possible technology initiative:

  ○ **"Thinks like me" voting recommendations.** With this idea, voters could register at DG and fill out a voting attitudes profile where they respond to questions that determine their core principles and point of view on government and political issues, such as the tradeoff between caring for the disadvantaged versus requiring citizens to be responsible for their own well-being and how much of a role the government should play in managing the economy. The questions would be designed (and continuously reevaluated) to be optimal predictors of how individuals would vote if they had studied and voted on particular issues. The system would look at voters who cast preliminary votes on the DG website as the basis for the predictions. Then, other voters who come to the DG website can see how voters who have similar values and attitudes have voted, with both a graphic and numeric indication of the statistical accuracy of the prediction. This will make it easier for some people who have not kept up with recent political discussion to find out how to cast votes that are likely to match how they would have voted if they had time to research the issues and candidates. Also, the technologies used would also carry over into some of the distant future ideas described in the next section.

IDEAS FOR THE DISTANT FUTURE

The blueprint for DG is much clearer in the near-term, more fuzzy in the long-term, and consists merely of some brainstorm sketches for the distant future.

Here are "out there" ideas that certainly would not happen for a long time, and likely never, but nevertheless I list these to spur creative thought about how to leverage technology and new social norms for moving mankind toward more responsive governance and, in some cases, toward true democracy:

- **An innovative polling approach that leverages "thinks like me" technologies.** This would work by having DG conduct a poll of voters about their opinions on particular issues while at the same time asking questions about core political philosophy. For example, a poll on an issue related to a specific piece of education law might also ask questions about core principles on the role of government in education (whether national government should have strong or weak control over curriculums, whether public education should be free through college/university, the role of religion). Then, DG would use statistical algorithms to find the correlation between specific policy questions and core principles. If the correlation is strong enough, then DG could publish statistical predictions about voter preference even when most voters are uninformed about a particular piece of legislation. This voter preference technology would probably take years to flesh out sufficiently such that it proves useful in practice. If/when this technology actually works, then DG can publish articles about what the people want on particular legislative issues at any granularity (national, state/province, local), and then inform the public whether a particular elected representative is honoring the will of his constituents.

- **An innovative new form of political party** where elected representatives always vote and act to reflect the will of his/her constituents, rather than his/her personal views. (This initiative would be dependent on the previous bullet, or some other similar technology that can determine voter preference automatically.) Some of the key aspects:

  ◦ Candidates would promise (contractually bound) to vote and act according to the consensus view of constituents, where constituent opinions are weighted by the constituent's trustworthiness score.

  ◦ Like DG itself, everything about the party is documented and made public in real time. Absolutely no secrets and not even the hint of dishonesty or corruption.

  ◦ The candidate's primary job is to educate constituents what votes are coming up and where to find information to learn and form an opinion. The DG would provide each candidate and elected official with state-of-the-art technology around real-time legislative activities and governance.

  ◦ DG candidates do not attempt to win votes based on the candidate's views; instead, campaign on expected effectiveness irrespective of particular views.

- **Electronic voting** – either at home or voting station

- DG could take a leadership role to make safe, secure and verifiable electronic voting a reality. One of the requirements would be that every aspect of electronic voting is transparent and completely auditable by any citizen. The verifiability will be the most time-consuming aspect of the enterprise.

- Modern online user experience optimized for tablets and phone presents issues and arguments

- Because it's online, issue discussion and arguments will be improved

  - Won't be restricted by number of words (which is necessary for printed voter pamphlets)

  - Any number of pro/con debates (whereas printed voter pamphlets in California only have a single pro/con debate on printed voter pamphlets)

  - People who view the discussion and arguments can use social media techniques such as ratings and comments about whether the content is helpful. This info will be integrated with "voters like me" technology so that voters can quickly sort through arguments to find those arguments that match their point of view

  - Discussion and arguments can include graphics, video and audio

- Security would be provided by future biometric

devices [1] and/or security chips embedded in these computing devices. [2][3]

- **"Voters like me"** and **proxy voting**

  - "Voters like me" are determined by best matching your past electronic votes with other people's past votes and best matching your views on the country's most polarizing issues with other people's views

  - In addition to "voters like me", voters can also see similar information about voters like someone else (e.g., a celebrity, your pastor, a particular blogger) if that person allows others to see such information

  - The voting software will also show the aggregate averages for people who have already cast votes so voters can get a sense for the emerging consensus

  - These techniques help voters who are actually casting votes to understand the issues and to sort through arguments much more quickly than today because you can quickly see how people with similar points of view have analyzed the issue and what percentage of people like you have already voted one way or another

  - These techniques enable proxy voting where your point of view will be counted in the vote totals even if you don't find the time to vote directly. Proxy voting uses a computing algorithm that assigns fractional votes based on how people like you voted.

- ○ Proxy votes might count 0.75 vs. direct votes (1.0) to encourage people to vote directly

- **Direct voting replaces representative voting** on most issues:

  - ○ California's current proposition voting system (direct voting on laws) is the starting point, but enhanced:

    - electronic voting

    - proxy voting

    - also used for elections

  - ○ Elected representatives ultimately would vote only on issues not suitable for direct election methods, such as some elements of budgeting and things mandated by constitution (e.g., treaty approvals, judge appointment approvals)

  - ○ Elected representatives would be expected to take active roles in holding hearings and authoring propositions that are then voted on by the people

I invite all people who have a passion for democracy to think big about what steps we can take together, taking advantage of whatever tools lie before us, whether they are the passions of the people, new technologies or anything else. Whatever the methods, we the people need to come together to ensure that we govern ourselves long into the future.

8 Conclusion - Calls to Action

Confidence and enthusiasm for democracy are at dangerously low levels. [1] The Western world has been shaken by an assault on truth, partly by selfish interests such as Russia who feel that they will benefit the more that Western democracies stumble or even collapse. (See Chapter 2: An Age-Old Conflict.) The big worry is that once democracies collapse, they may never come back because autocratic governments now have the technology to establish a police state. (See Chapter 3: Threat of Big Brother.)

I define the aspirational ideal of True Democracy as:

- Every single adult citizen has the right to vote
- Citizenship is available on an equal basis to all adults

regardless of race, ethnicity, gender, economic status or political inclination so long as the given adult meets a set of fair citizenship criteria that are not prejudicial against any particular group

- Citizens vote directly on elected government positions (e.g., President) and on legislation, rather than indirectly via elected representatives (i.e., direct democracy)

- All citizens are fully informed by science-based and objective facts and analysis. Commercial and political special interests are not able to manipulate the views of the voters except through fact-based information that simultaneously shows all sides of the discussion fairly and respectfully.

Representative democracies, such as we have in the world today, are vulnerable to manipulation by the powerful few. (See Chapter 4: True Democracy.) A skillful demagogue can take advantage of a crisis, real or manufactured, to convince citizens to gradually relinquish democratic rights and freedoms until the demagogue has absolute power, which he enforces using modern technology via a police state and invasive surveillance.

I call on all people with a passion for self-government to put aside ideological differences and overcome complacency to mobilize together to fight the very real threats before us. Mankind has rallied before. (See Chapter 5: Holy War)

I call for a nonprofit, Democracy Guardians (DG), that would create a world-class database of people and organizations that are sources of information on government and politics, and then do the following (see Chapter 6: Prioritizing Trustworthiness):

- Collect trustworthiness reviews and rating scores on these people and organizations by trusted and trained DG members, and store them in the cloud with full transparency on every aspect of its operations

- Compute two numeric values for each Internet ID (person or organization): an average trustworthiness rating and a confidence value on that rating

- Generate a small icon that conveys at a glance the trustworthiness of a particular individual or organization

- Work with the media and news aggregators to show the trustworthiness icon next to the byline of news articles so that readers can see at a glance the trustworthiness of the author (person or organization)

- Promote the service so that its use is widespread, and thereby pressure government, politicians, the media and pundits to be more honest and complete in their communications. The fear of being branded as untrustworthy would discourage politicians, pundits and the media from posting untruths or distorted reporting.

DG would be a global nonpartisan organization that would channel the passions of people who share a vision for self-government. The organization would strengthen democratic institutions, and thereby promote governments that serve the people, not the other way around. In addition to its trustworthiness initiative, DG would look at various education and evangelism initiatives that are consistent with its mission. To fortify itself against selfish forces that might want to discredit DG because they want to promote false propaganda for money or power reasons, DG will build organizational strength on multiple fronts, including financial, educational and legal. Over the long term, DG will likely pursue various technology initiatives beyond its trustworthiness platform which would help move the world towards the ideals and principles described in this book. (See Chapter 7: Towards True Democracy.)

Some in the West worry that democracy is fragile and subject to authoritarian takeover. I belong to that group for reasons I explained in the Threat of Big Brother chapter. I feel that those who are passionate about democratic government need to come together in a sort of Holy War to preserve existing democracies. But I don't believe defense is enough to counter the existential threats, let alone fix democracy's many shortcomings that I outlined in the True Democracy chapter. I believe that democracy patriots need to go on the offense to improve democracy, using the power of passion and technology.

End Notes

1 HAS DEMOCRACY LOST ITS FERVOR?

1. "Presidential Priority: Restore American Leadership", World Affairs, Spring 2016, Eliot Cohen, Eric S. Edelman and Brian Hook, http://www.worldaffairsjournal.org/article/presidential-priority-restore-american-leadership

2. "Have leading democracies 'lost their moral fervor'?", http://www.demdigest.org/leading-democracies-lost-moral-fervor.

3. "Freedom in the World 2016", Freedom House, https://freedomhouse.org/sites/default/files/FH_FITW_Report_2016.pdf.

4. "How Stable Are Democracies? Warning Signs Are Flashing Red' ", Amanda Taub, New York Times,

2016,https://www.nytimes.com/2016/11/
29/world/americas/western-liberal-
democracy.html?_r=0.

2 AN AGE-OLD CONFLICT

1. "At 2.6 million strong, Women's Marches
   crush expectations", USA Today, 2017,
   http://www.usatoday.com/story/news/
   politics/2017/01/21/womens-march-aims-
   start-movement-trump-inauguration/
   96864158/.
2. "Who started the march? One woman",
   Los Angeles Times, 2017,
   http://www.latimes.com/nation/la-na-pol-
   womens-march-live-who-started-the-
   march-one-1485033621-htmlstory.html.
3. "Fake News Expert On How False Stories
   Spread And Why People Believe Them",
   http://www.npr.org/2016/12/14/
   505547295/fake-news-expert-on-how-
   false-stories-spread-and-why-people-
   believe-them.
4. Fake News: How a Partying Macedonian
   Teen Earns Thousands Publishing Lies",
   http://www.nbcnews.com/news/world/
   fake-news-how-partying-macedonian-
   teen-earns-thousands-publishing-lies-
   n692451.

5. "How Teens In The Balkans Are Duping Trump Supporters With Fake News", https://www.buzzfeed.com/craigsilverman/how-macedonia-became-a-global-hub-for-pro-trump-misinfo?utm_term=.vw7eXjazba#.lo9WRyx20x.

6. "Trump Calls the News Media the 'Enemy of the American People'", New York Times, 2017, https://www.nytimes.com/2017/02/17/business/trump-calls-the-news-media-the-enemy-of-the-people.html.

7. "Russian propaganda effort helped spread 'fake news' during election, experts say", Washington Post, 2016, https://www.washingtonpost.com/business/economy/russian-propaganda-effort-helped-spread-fake-news-during-election-experts-say/2016/11/24/793903b6-8a40-4ca9-b712-716af66098fe_story.html?utm_term=.d263363ea31.

8. "Donald Trump again claims to have largest presidential inauguration audience in history", Independent, 2017, http://www.independent.co.uk/news/world/americas/donald-trump-claims-presidential-inuauguration-audience-

history-us-president-white-house-barack-a7547141.html.

9. "Donald Trump had biggest inaugural crowd ever? Metrics don't show it", PolitiFact, 2017, http://www.politifact.com/truth-o-meter/statements/2017/jan/21/sean-spicer/trump-had-biggest-inaugural-crowd-ever-metrics-don/.

10. "Conway: Trump White House offered 'alternative facts' on crowd size", CNN, 2017, http://www.cnn.com/2017/01/22/politics/kellyanne-conway-alternative-facts/.

11. "Nine years of censorship", Nature, 2016, http://www.nature.com/news/nine-years-of-censorship-1.19842.

12. "Women's suffrage", Wikipedia, https://en.wikipedia.org/wiki/Women's_suffrage.

13. "Dialectic", Wikipedia, https://en.wikipedia.org/wiki/Dialectic.

3 THREAT OF BIG BROTHER

1. "George Orwell's '1984' Is Suddenly a Best-Seller", New York Times, https://www.nytimes.com/2017/01/25/

books/1984-george-orwell-donald-trump.html.

2. "The NSA notes", The Guardian, https://www.theguardian.com/us-news/the-nsa-files.

3. "NSA tapped German Chancellery for decades, WikiLeaks claims", The Guardian, https://www.theguardian.com/us-news/2015/jul/08/nsa-tapped-german-chancellery-decades-wikileaks-claims-merkel.

4. "XKeyscore: NSA tool collects 'nearly everything a user does on the internet'", tapnewswire.com, http://tapnewswire.com/2013/07/i-sitting-at-my-desk-said-snowden-could.

5. 'No Place to Hide' by Glenn Greenwald, on the NSA's sweeping efforts to 'Know it All", Washington Post, https://www.washingtonpost.com/opinions/no-place-to-hide-by-glenn-greenwald-on-the-nsas-sweeping-efforts-to-know-it-all/2014/05/12/dfa45dee-d628-11e3-8a78-8fe50322a72c_story.html?utm_term=.1a801dfc39d6.

6. U. S. Patriot Act, 2001, https://www.gpo.gov/fdsys/pkg/

PLAW-107publ56/html/
PLAW-107publ56.htm.

7. "Tech Companies Concede to Surveillance Program", New York Times, http://www.nytimes.com/2013/06/08/technology/tech-companies-bristling-concede-to-government-surveillance-efforts.html.

8. "The price of free: how Apple, Facebook, Microsoft and Google sell you to advertisers", PC World, 2015, http://www.pcworld.com/article/2986988/privacy/the-price-of-free-how-apple-facebook-microsoft-and-google-sell-you-to-advertisers.html.

9. "One surveillance camera for every 11 people in Britain, says CCTV survey", The Telegraph, 2013, http://www.telegraph.co.uk/technology/10172298/One-surveillance-camera-for-every-11-people-in-Britain-says-CCTV-survey.html.

10. "WHERE DO TERRORISTS COME FROM? NOT THE NATIONS NAMED IN TRUMP BAN", Newsweek, 2017, http://www.newsweek.com/where-do-terrorists-come-not-seven-countries-named-550581.

11. "Causes of World War I", Wikipedia, https://en.wikipedia.org/wiki/ Causes_of_World_War_I.

12. "German Nationalism", Wikipedia, https://en.wikipedia.org/wiki/ German_nationalism# 1933-1945_under_Nazi_Germany.

13. "Gestapo",Wikipedia, https://en.wikipedia.org/wiki/Gestapo.

14. "The Holocaust", Wikipedia, https://en.wikipedia.org/wiki/ The_Holocaust.

15. "What Is Fascism?", John T. Flynn, Miles Institute, 2008, https://mises.org/library/ what-fascism.

16. "German resistance to Nazism", Wikipedia, https://en.wikipedia.org/wiki/ German_resistance_to_Nazism.

17. "Intelligence Report: On Putin's Orders, Russia Sought to Influence Presidential Election", US News and World Report, 2017, https://www.usnews.com/news/ world/articles/2017-01-06/intelligence- report-on-vladimir-putins-orders-russia- sought-to-influence-presidential-election.

18. "Russia accused of waging secret warfare against Britain using cyber attacks, espionage and fake news", The Telegraph,

2016, http://www.telegraph.co.uk/news/
2016/12/17/russia-accused-waging-secret-
war-against-britain-using-cyber.

19. "Russia engineered election hacks and
meddling in Europe", US News and World
Report, 2017,http://www.usatoday.com/
story/news/world/2017/01/09/russia-
engineered-election-hacks-europe/
96216556/.

20. "The scary truth about what Putin really
wants (and Obama's willful ignorance)",
Judith Miller, Fox News Opinion, 2016,
http://www.foxnews.com/opinion/2016/
10/08/scary-truth-about-what-putin-
really-wants-and-obama-s-willful-
ignorance.html.

21. "What Does Russian President Vladimir
Putin Want?", US News and World
Report, 2016, https://www.usnews.com/
opinion/op-ed/articles/2016-12-27/what-
does-russian-president-vladimir-putin-
want.

22. "How the Civil War Changed the
World", Don Doyle, *The New York Times
Disunion The History of the Civil War*,
Oxford University Press, 2016, edited by
Ted Widmer.

23. "These 8 men are richer than 3.6 billion

people combined", CNN,
http://money.cnn.com/2017/01/15/news/
economy/oxfam-income-inequality-men/.

24. "These 6 Corporations Control 90% Of
The Media In America", Business Insider,
2012, http://www.businessinsider.com/
these-6-corporations-control-90-of-the-
media-in-america-2012-6.

25. "Trump's Koch administration", Politico,
2016, http://www.politico.com/story/2016/
11/trump-koch-brothers-231863.

26. "What a Trump America Can Learn from
a Berlusconi Italy", New York Times,
2016, https://www.nytimes.com/2016/11/
16/opinion/what-a-trump-america-can-
learn-from-a-berlusconi-italy.html.

27. "New Erdogan powers 'huge threat' to
democracy, warns HRW", The New Arab,
2017, https://www.alaraby.co.uk/english/
news/2017/1/18/new-erdogan-powers-
huge-threat-to-democracy-warns-hrw.

28. "This Stunningly Racist French Novel Is
How Steve Bannon Explains The World",
The Huffington Post, 2017,
http://www.huffingtonpost.com/entry/
steve-bannon-camp-of-the-saints-
immigration_us_58b75206e4b0284854b3dc03.

29. "2016 Was the Hottest Year on Record",

Scientific American, 2017,
https://www.scientificamerican.com/
article/2016-was-the-hottest-year-on-
record.

30. "Sea Temperature Rise", National
Geographic,
http://ocean.nationalgeographic.com/
ocean/explore/pristine-seas/critical-issues-
sea-temperature-rise/.

31. "Arctic ice melt could trigger
uncontrollable climate change at global
level", The Guardian, 2016,
https://www.theguardian.com/
environment/2016/nov/25/arctic-ice-melt-
trigger-uncontrollable-climate-change-
global-level.

32. "Scientists nearly double sea level rise
projections for 2100, because of
Antarctica", Washington Post, 2016,
https://www.washingtonpost.com/news/
energy-environment/wp/2016/03/30/
antarctic-loss-could-double-expected-sea-
level-rise-by-2100-scientists-
say/?tid=a_inl&utm_term=.dab641900a3.

33. Trevor M Letcher, "Climate Change:
Observed impacts on Planet Earth", 2009,
https://www.amazon.com/Climate-

Change-Observed-impacts-Planet/dp/
044453301X.

34. "Carbon Dioxide Absorption in the Near
Infrared", Jordan Werbe-fuentes, Michael
Moody, Oriana Korol, Tristan Kading,
http://jvarekamp.web.wesleyan.edu/CO2/
FP-1.pdf.

35. "Is the current level of atmospheric CO2
concentration unprecedented in Earth's
history?", The Royal Society,
https://royalsociety.org/topics-policy/
projects/climate-change-evidence-causes/
question-7.

36. "The Carbon Dioxide Greenhouse
Effect", American Institute of Physics,
2017, http://history.aip.org/climate/
co2.htm.

37. "Ice Core Data Help Solve a Global
Warming Mystery", Scientific American,
2013, https://www.scientificamerican.com/
article/ice-core-data-help-solve.

38. "Temperatures from Fossil Shells",
American Institute of Physics, 2012,
http://history.aip.org/climate/forams.htm.

39. "Mother of pearl holds data about ancient
ocean temperatures", Natural World, 2016,
https://www.theweathernetwork.com/

news/articles/mother-of-pearl-holds-data-about-ancient-ocean-temperatures-/7710.

40. "Stem-cell pioneer blamed media 'bashing' in suicide note", Nature, 2014, http://www.nature.com/news/stem-cell-pioneer-blamed-media-bashing-in-suicide-note-1.15715.

41. Cook, John; Oreskes, Naomi; Doran, Peter T.; Anderegg, William R. L.; Verheggen, Bart; Maibach, Ed W.; Carlton, J. Stuart; Lewandowsky, Stephan; Skuce, Andrew G.; Green, Sarah A. (2016), "Consensus on consensus: a synthesis of consensus estimates on human-caused global warming", Environmental Research Letters, 11 (44), doi:10.1088/1748-9326/11/4/, http://iopscience.iop.org/article/10.1088/1748-9326/11/4/048002/meta

42. "Bangladesh faces climate change refugee nightmare", Reuters, 2008, http://www.reuters.com/article/us-bangladesh-climate-islands-idUSDHA23447920080414.

43. "Scientists highlight deadly health risks of climate change", CNN, 2017, http://www.cnn.com/2017/02/16/health/climate-change-deaths-health-al-gore-bn/.

4 TRUE DEMOCRACY

1. Aristotle, Politics.1317b (Book 6, Part II), http://www.perseus.tufts.edu/hopper/text?doc=Perseus%3Atext%3A1999.01.0058%3Abook%3D6%3Asection%3D1317b.

2. "Freedom in the World 2016", Freedom House, https://freedomhouse.org/sites/default/files/FH_FITW_Report_2016.pdf.

3. "Scott Pelley: Fake news, biased reporting a threat to our country", Arizona State University Senate, 2016, https://usenate.asu.edu/scott-pelley-fake-news-biased-reporting-threat-our-country.

4. "Why Redistricting Threatens Democracy", The Nation, 2012, https://www.thenation.com/article/why-redistricting-threatens-democracy/.

5. "Republicans were wildly successful at suppressing voters in 2016", Think Progress, 2016, https://thinkprogress.org/2016-a-case-study-in-voter-suppression-258b5f90ddcd#.17nui7dp.

6. "California ballot proposition", Wikipedia, https://en.wikipedia.org/wiki/California_ballot_proposition.

7. "Jimmy Carter Calls Campaign Finance Rules 'Legal Bribery'", Think Progress,

2016, http://time.com/4206347/jimmy-carter-campaign-finance-legal-bribery.

8. "Citizens United v. FEC", Wikipedia, https://en.wikipedia.org/wiki/Citizens_United_v._FEC.

9. "Koch network pledges to defend Republicans who vote against GOP health bill", Politico, 2017, http://www.politico.com/story/2017/03/koch-brothers-obamacare-house-republicans-236389.

10. "Views on Gun Control: A Polling Summary (POLL)", ABC News, 2016, http://abcnews.go.com/Politics/views-gun-control-polling-summary-poll/story?id=36096424.

11. "NRA threatens to punish lawmakers on gun control vote despite deal", NBC News, 2013, http://nbcpolitics.nbcnews.com/_news/2013/04/10/17694499-nra-threatens-to-punish-lawmakers-on-gun-control-vote-despite-deal?lite.

12. "How the NRA wields its influence",CNN,2013, http://www.cnn.com/2013/01/09/us/nra-gun-research/.

13. "AARP Is Killing Entitlement Reform",

Spectator, 2011, https://spectator.org/
36763_aarp-killing-entitlement-reform/.

14. "Trump orders lobbying restrictions on
ex-officials", USA Today, 2017,
http://www.usatoday.com/story/news/
politics/2017/01/28/donald-trump-ethics-
lawyers-barack-obama/97187656/.

15. "527 organization", Wikipedia,
https://en.wikipedia.org/wiki/
527_organization.

16. "These 15 Billionaires Own America's
News Media Companies", Forbes, 2016,
http://www.forbes.com/sites/katevinton/
2016/06/01/these-15-billionaires-own-
americas-news-media-
companies/#325e0ba130b.

17. "DECLASSIFIED: Read the intelligence
report on Russia interfering with US
election", CNBC, 2016,
http://www.cnbc.com/2017/01/06/
intelligence-community-says-putin-
ordered-campaign-to-influence-election-
denigrate-clinton.html.

18. "Why you believe everything your
Facebook friends tell you", CNN, 2016,
http://www.cnn.com/2016/10/19/health/
facebook-friends-hoaxes.

19. "Facebook is helping to power Trump —

and his rivals", CNN, 2017, http://www.cnn.com/2017/03/15/opinions/power-of-facebook-on-politics-opinion-srinivasan/index.html.

20. "Political parties in the United States", Wikipedia, https://en.wikipedia.org/wiki/Political_parties_in_the_United_States.

21. "The Founding Fathers Tried to Warn Us About the Threat From a Two-Party System", Washingtons Blog, 2011, http://www.washingtonsblog.com/2011/07/the-founding-fathers-tried-to-warn-us-about-the-threat-from-a-two-party-system.html.

22. "Scott Pelley: Fake news, biased reporting a threat to our country", Arizona State University Senate, 2016, https://usenate.asu.edu/scott-pelley-fake-news-biased-reporting-threat-our-country.

5 HOLY WAR

1. "Latin American wars of independence", Wikipedia, https://en.wikipedia.org/wiki/Latin_American_wars_of_independence.

2. "World War 2 Statistics, http://www.secondworldwarhistory.com/world-war-2-statistics.asp.

3. "Top inventions and technical innovations

of World War 2", Chris Finnamore and David Ludlow, 2015, http://www.expertreviews.co.uk/technology/7907/top-inventions-and-technical-innovations-of-world-war-2.

4. "The Greatest Generation", Tom Brokaw, 1998, http://www.penguinrandomhouse.com/books/18729/the-greatest-generation-by-tom-brokaw/9781400063147.

5. "List of wars and anthropogenic disasters by death toll", Wikipedia, https://en.wikipedia.org/wiki/List_of_wars_and_anthropogenic_disasters_by_death_toll.

6. "United Nations", Wikipedia, https://en.wikipedia.org/wiki/United_Nations.

7. "NATO", Wikipedia, https://en.wikipedia.org/wiki/NATO#Members.

8. "World Bank", Wikipedia, https://en.wikipedia.org/wiki/World_Bank.

9. "Marshall Plan", Wikipedia, https://en.wikipedia.org/wiki/Marshall_Plan.

10. "International Court of Justice",

Wikipedia, https://en.wikipedia.org/wiki/
International_Court_of_Justice.

11. "International Monetary Fund",
Wikipedia, https://en.wikipedia.org/wiki/
International_Monetary_Fund.

12. "General Agreement on Tariffs and
Trade", Wikipedia,
https://en.wikipedia.org/wiki/
General_Agreement_on_Tariffs_and_Trade.

13. "Organization of American States",
Wikipedia, https://en.wikipedia.org/wiki/
Organization_of_American_States.

14. "Bretton Woods", Wikipedia,
https://en.wikipedia.org/wiki/
Bretton_Woods_system.

15. "Adolf Hitler's rise to power", Wikipedia,
https://en.wikipedia.org/wiki/
Adolf_Hitler%27s_rise_to_power.

16. "Did Celebrity Endorsements Contribute
to Hillary Clinton's Presidential Upset?",
Vanity Fair, 2016,
http://www.vanityfair.com/style/2016/11/
celebrity-endorsements-donald-trump-
hillary-clinton.

6 PRIORITIZING TRUSTWORTHINESS

1. McKenna, Regis, *Relationship Marketing*,
New York: Addison-Wesley, 1991, p. 96,

https://www.amazon.com/Relationship-Marketing-Successful-Strategies-Customer/dp/0201622408.

2. Kang, Karen, *BrandingPays: The Five-Step System to Reinvent Your Personal Brand*, 2013, p. 108, https://www.amazon.com/BrandingPays-Five-Step-System-Reinvent-Personal/dp/0988437503/ref=tmm_hrd_swatch_0?_encoding=UTF8&qid=1488580151&sr=1-1. Figure from Kang's book adapted for this book with her permission.

3. "Halo effect", Britannica, https://www.britannica.com/topic/halo-effect.

4. http://blacklivesmatter.com/.

5. "Here Are The Most- And Least-Trusted News Outlets In America", Pamela Engel, Business Insider, 2014, http://www.businessinsider.com/here-are-the-most-and-least-trusted-news-outlets-in-america-2014-10.

6. "Intelligence Agencies Say Russia Ordered 'Influence Campaign' to Aid Donald Trump in Election", Wall Street Journal, 2017, https://www.wsj.com/articles/donald-trump-continues-attacks-on-

intelligence-agencies-ahead-of-classified-briefing-on-russia-1483728966.

7. "Russia accused of waging secret warfare against Britain using cyber attacks, espionage and fake news", The Telegraph, 2016, http://www.telegraph.co.uk/news/2016/12/17/russia-accused-waging-secret-war-against-britain-using-cyber.

8. "Facebook Partners With Fact-Checkers to Fight Fake News", Rolling Stone, 2016, http://www.rollingstone.com/politics/news/facebook-partners-with-fact-checkers-to-fight-fake-news-w456268.

9. http://graphics.wsj.com/blue-feed-red-feed/#/guns.

10. "GOP Specifically Stated They Wanted Obama To Fail And Would Obstruct At Every Turn", EGBERTO WILLIES, 2012, https://egbertowillies.com/2012/09/02/gop-specifically-stated-they-wanted-obama-to-fail-and-would-obstruct-at-every-turn/.

11. "When did McConnell say he wanted to make Obama a 'one-term president'?", Washington Post, 2012, https://www.washingtonpost.com/blogs/fact-checker/post/when-did-mcconnell-say-he-wanted-to-make-obama-a-one-term-president/2012/09/24/

79fd5cd8-0696-11e2-afff-
d6c7f20a83bf_blog.html?utm_term=
.dfd7400f496.

12. "Reminder Obamacare passed without a
single Republican vote", Oregon Catalyst,
2013, http://oregoncatalyst.com/
25561-reminder-obamacare-passed-single-
republican-vote.html.

13. "The Power Of Culture As A
Competitive Advantage", Forbes, 2015,
https://www.forbes.com/sites/yec/2015/09/
15/the-power-of-culture-as-a-
competitive-advantage/#28b0de823f6b.

7 TOWARDS TRUE DEMOCRACY

1. "Biometrics: The future of digital security",
Luke Graham, CNBC, 2016,
http://www.cnbc.com/2016/04/05/
biometrics-future-of-digital-cyber-
security.html.

2. "Security at W3C", https://www.w3.org/
Security/.

3. "HARDWARE BASED SECURE
SERVICES COMMUNITY GROUP",
https://www.w3.org/community/hb-
secure-services/.

8 CONCLUSION – CALLS TO ACTION

1. "How Stable Are Democracies? Warning Signs Are Flashing Red' ", Amanda Taub, New York Times, 2016,https://www.nytimes.com/2016/11/29/world/americas/western-liberal-democracy.html?_r=0.

Acknowledgements

The author thanks the people who reviewed and gave helpful feedback on early drafts, starting with my daughter Nikki, who has so many talents and so much understanding; my sister Dr. Bobbe Ferraiolo, who was both so helpful and supportive; Nikki's husband Taunton Paine, who is a treasure trove of history and current events; my daughters Allison and Dr. Natalie for their love, encouragement and the millennial perspective; and my brother-in-law Steve Kang for great feedback and keeping me aware of events in academia. Thanks to Dragan Bilic, who was a pleasure to work with on the cover art. Thanks to my greater family and my many friends for the support and generosity they have given me as I face my physical decline. Finally, greatest thanks to my wife, Karen Kang, the guru of personal branding, who keeps me happy and comfortable, gives me great feedback and advice, manages my care, takes care of house and puppy, supports us by working and puts love in my life.

I also want to thank all the people who trailblazed accessibility standards, laws and products so that I have the ability to live a very good life even as my physical abilities decline. In particular, the entire book was authored with eye gaze technology from Tobii Dynavox. And thanks to the various passionate people in the ALS community for working tirelessly towards cure and comfort for people like me.

How To Help

If you like the ideas from this book and want to help, please go to http://DemocracyGuardians.org, where you can donate and find out how to get involved.

Proceeds

All net proceeds from this book will be given to Democracy Guardians or other nonprofits which share the vision of improving democracy so that it truly delivers on the promise of the people, by the people and for the people, instead of government by the powerful few.

Made in the USA
Lexington, KY
30 May 2017